AGING-itis
How to Be Happy Despite It All

By
Rima Rudner

*Dedicated to everyone that has
stuck with me through thick and thin.
Harvey, Lulu, Lara, Stacey
Betsy, Sandi, Bonnie, Lois
Suzanne, Ivy, Jan, Don
Linda and Dan
Johanna and Paul
Gloria and Harvey
Beth and Alfie
Harvey and Susan
And all the rest of you.
You know who you are.*

Contents

CHAPTER ONE
How to Survive "The Big Mess"

No ONE, YES, *that's no one*, has the right to make your life unhappy!" Are you fighting negative thoughts no matter how hard you try to be happy? Do you worry too much or have fears you know you should overcome? Does listening to the news make you feel like it's only doom and gloom? Do you feel tired, depressed, and sick of it all? Do you feel aches and pains you've never had before? Well baby, you're not alone. Millions of people like you are experiencing *Aging-itis*. It's a condition of getting older in this post pandemic world that seems like it's spinning out of control.

People are going nuts! Hate and anger have turned into mass shootings and stabbings. Extremist groups want to destroy our country. Homelessness and crime have turned our streets into killing fields. Greed and power have destroyed our morals and ethics. Truths have turned into lies. Our children are committing suicide or overdosing on fentanyl. Declining social-ization has caused a loneliness epidemic. The mental health of our country is deteriorating quickly as we watch it happen before our eyes. Wars have annihi-lated countries and people are starving even in rich nations. The rich and powerful grow stronger while we watch them flaunt it. Entertaining, but infuriating. Logic has all but disappeared. I call this "The Big Mess." How are you supposed to be happy aging in a world like this? *You can! Read on…*

My obsession about finding happiness was born out of being an unhappy little girl that wanted to commit suicide by the time she was five years old. I craved happiness so much that I turned it into my life's work. In my previous book, "Choose to Be Happy: A Guide to Total Happiness," I was able to prove that happiness comes partly from our genetics and partly from nurture. Happiness is an attitude about what happens to us that we can acquire at any age. We can *brainwash* ourselves to be happy no matter what happens in our lives and in the world. I will show you how to do it.

My search for happiness and my resilience to overcome my pain and any and all obstacles has led me to write this book for you. I've survived cancer, serious illnesses, and whatever roadblocks life has to hand out. I've gone from riches to rags, to survival mode, but my resilience and humor have led me to the secret of staying joyful and still being able to laugh and have fun no matter what happens. I hope you will laugh at my humor, enjoy my funny life experiences, learn from my wisdom, marvel at my resilience, and find more strength within yourselves from my stories and insight.

The Journey Begins

Whoa! What's Happening? I thought as I made the bumpy ride out of this slimy birth canal, through a forest of black curly pubic hair, and into these gigantic thingies that I later learned were hands. *What the hell was going on?* Someone grabbed me by my feet, turned me upside down, and started slapping me on my back as if I had swallowed a ping-pong ball. I had been perfectly content floating around in that stuff I found out later was amniotic fluid, which sounds like an additive to keep your car from rusting. I started crying, *For God sakes do something!* I was covered with this gooey stuff. They cleaned me up and laid me on this big fleshy stomach and it soothed me. Everything looked cloudy (kind of like now, but that's just from cataracts). I saw this woman's face looking down at me as if to say, "Maybe she'll get prettier." Next to her stood a tall red-haired man with big ears glaring down at me as if saying "Oy, another f--king kid", so it must have been my father. Then I saw a couple of frowning women in white uniforms and this man in a white coat with this rubber snake-like thingy hanging around his neck. *Where the hell was I? Who was I? How did I get here?* Who were all these people? I was so confused. Was this the beginning of my life? If so, it was going to be a one hell of a scary rollercoaster ride.

My mother used to tell me, "You woke up on the wrong side of the bed", so I took my little twin bed and pushed one side against the wall. I wanted to wake up happy. I've always wanted to wake up happy. I've been through a lot in my life, a lot of fun, happiness, love, but also a lot of sadness, emotional and physical pain, and a lot of illness. I've had more surgeries than I can count, but that's because I'm not that great at math anymore. I can't find a part of my body that hasn't been operated on except for my brain, and that's still very much intact. In order to find happiness, I've had to learn that we all need to laugh a lot and not to take life so seriously. What seems so bad while we're going through it is usually what we can laugh about tomorrow.

Sure, these are challenging times, but all times have been difficult in some ways. I promised myself I wouldn't get political because I didn't want to get murdered by some radical, so let's just say the world is divided now and the forces of good and evil have gotten stronger. There are many shades of good and evil, so I like to just call them Team Good and Team Evil and make it a game. Team Evil thinks good people are evil, and Team Good thinks that evil people are evil. If this upside-down logic persists, we're all going to hell in a handbag anyway, so let's make it a designer bag and live life to the fullest.

Many of us are on edge because our sense of security has been threatened with global warming and an increasing crime rate. Let's face it, the world is a mess right now. I call it "The Big Mess". We worry about inflation, our health, our planet, war, and our freedom. I was born with the worry gene and am a "What If?" person. If there's nothing to worry about, I worry about having nothing to worry about. Luckily, I've learned how to find humor in everything because worry and negativity achieves nothing and creates facial lines and I want to save money on Botox. If you hear that the planet killer asteroid is going to hit your neighborhood, just get drunk and eat all of the fattening foods you love, or just drive to another neighborhood.

I used to be so unhappy that when I was a little girl that I read Sylvia Plath poems and contemplated killing myself all the time. I'd lie down on the grass outside in the dark and stare at the stars for hours getting eaten by mosquitos, trying to figure out the meaning of life. I finally did. We are put on this earth to maintain its beauty, make ourselves happy, make other people happy, and to leave the earth a better place to live in for the next generation.

I've also figured out our Creator's gameplan. Two people have sex and plant a seed, kind of like planting a summer squash, then there is birth, a new little summer squash is born, and life begins, like when the Universe was born, the Big Bang. This was really the beginning of our journey, and the game is to add something good to our world before we made it to the finish line.

I've also learned that surviving in this world involves understanding the Game of Life our Creator dreamt up to amuse himself, or herself, or itself, or however you envision our Creator.

As I've aged, I've realized that life is a chess game between Team Good, which wants to make the world a happy place, and Team Evil, which wants to destroy our world and our happiness. That's just the way life is. Our Creator is the divine puppeteer pulling the strings, and we are the marionettes singing and dancing around on our stupid looking wooden legs. Our Creator is authoring the supreme novel and no one, yes no one, not even our Creator knows how it is going to end. It could be tomorrow, or it could be billions of years away. Life is the ultimate page-turner and that is what makes it so difficult and yet so much fun. I just can't figure out how our Creator keeps track of all our lives since there are almost eight billion people on this planet. Is there life on other planets? Do they have the same Creator? If so, our Creator must be *even busier* than all the politicians erasing all their texts and shredding their emails.

Once we emerge from our mothers' birth canals, our Creator turns on our timer, and our days are numbered. If we live to be one hundred, we've got over 36,500 days to fill up. You only live once (I think), but maybe our souls are reincarnated. As we age, we have less time left to deal with the sewage in our lives; every grain of sand that sifts through that glass sand timer represents a day that we can be happy or unhappy, laugh or not laugh. Life can be fun no matter how old we are. No matter what happens to us. Laugh at yourself, your life, the world, funny movies, everyday life, or anything that makes you laugh. Find humor wherever you can, even sex can be funny. Laughing is an orgasm for your soul.

CHAPTER TWO
How to Find the Humor in Aging

Iᴛ ᴡᴀꜱ ᴍʏ birthday and nothing worse could have happened than had already happened *I thought*. I went to the mailbox, pulled out a stack of birthday cards, mostly from the Neptune Society, wanting to sell me a cremation package. There was an envelope from, *I can't even say the word*, AARP, the American Association of Really Old People. I thought I was going to have an anxiety attack. It was that dreaded envelope that arrives in the mailbox of every United States citizen the day they turn fifty years old. I think the letter read, "You just turned fifty today, so let us ruin the rest of your life by cluttering it up with magazines you don't want to read, ads for mortuaries, and offers of free luggage you don't need." When I recovered from the shock, I did what every other sane person like me would do, I ran it through the shredder and then destroyed the whole shredder with a hammer. I was going to show them I wasn't an old, dilapidated person at fifty years old, so I dedicated the rest of my life to "The Joy of Aging" and went searching for a reason to live after receiving an AARP invitation. I figured it could be sex.

Sex for Seniors.

Contrary to what younger people think, older people do have sex, most commonly called "Don't Tell Our Kids". It involves ordering a lot of plain-wrapped boxes from questionable Internet sites after we've learned how to use the Internet without getting scammed. We also should have a partner, although this isn't really required. Then we must be up for some geriatric gymnastics because we really can't move with the same agility as when we were younger. I don't remember the last time I had sex, maybe it was last night, but my memory isn't so good anymore. I know I didn't have the Big Bang, so it must have been the Little Whimper, which is what I do when my hernia pops out.

My husband, Lou, can't remember if he saw a TV program before or not. He's watched every single Shark Tank episode since August 2009 ten times and still can't figure it out.

"Why are human beings sitting in chairs if they're sharks? he asks me.

"Because sharks are too slippery and slide off the chairs," I explain.

"Oh! I get it now," he replies as if he's just discovered the true meaning of life.

This is great because he can't remember whether we had sex last night or not. I lie and tell him we did, and it was the best sex I've ever had, so that makes him really happy. It feels good to make other people happy. Do it as often as you can, and the world will be a better place.

Sex is great as you get older if you can find a partner, and even if you can't, there are lots of online dating sites for older people. These sites are excellent if you don't mind taking the chance of falling in love with a serial killer or someone who's going to swindle all your money (*Clue: prison tattoos*) if you actually have any money left after you've spent the last few years buying stocks and fighting inflation. If you can't find someone on these sites, there are lots of toys for older people if you're not embarrassed to order them and can figure out how to use them. You might want to ask your mail carrier for help since they already saw the plain wrap box that was marked "Intimate Merchandise."

Actual sex is wonderful once you get going. (Men, be careful of taking sex performance drugs. One of the side effects is getting a painful prolonged erection, very embarrassing in the ER room or when your children are coming over for dinner.) We've decided to have sex in the daytime because neither one of us can stay up much longer past dinnertime. The problem with sex for older people is that when you've both got arthritis in your hips, knees, and hands, numb and tingling feet and legs, and herniated and bulging disks in your spine and neck, it's almost impossible to get into any position that doesn't make you scream in pain. The good news is that your partner and neighbors will think you're having a great orgasm.

Not having a partner can be a plus. All you must do is lay there and do your thing; no one else to have to please. The Catch-22 of aging is that women go into menopause at the average age of fifty-one years old and they no longer have periods, so they're free to have sex anytime when they're not kvetching about hot flashes and migraine headaches. Unfortunately, fifty-one-year-old men are about the age they start having erectile dysfunction, so there's a little compli-cation. Male and female blow-up dolls are a great solution. They make great dance partners too if you don't mind that they don't look like they're having an enjoyable time. Dancing is great for staying young and blow-up dolls won't argue with you, criticize your dancing, or step on your toes. It's easy to break up with them because you can stick them with a big needle and watch them pop.

One of the good things about getting older is that I don't worry about rape anymore. I've created my own rape kit. It consists of wrinkles, menopause, hemorrhoids, gastritis, no makeup, age-related hair loss, laxatives, and hanging boobs. My boobs have gotten so low now that I have to wear a belt around my waist to keep them from chafing my thighs.

Gravity

Our skin is as soft and smooth as a lambskin bag when we're born, but gravity pulls us down to the ground lower and lower until our skin looks like a wrinkled potato sack crumbled on the floor. I wanted to defy gravity, so I stood on my head, but I just got a bad migraine. One way to avoid looking old is to cover up all your mirrors. Orthodox Jews do that when they are in mourning, which is called sitting Shiva. This comes from the story of Moshe from New York who got so cold at funerals that he would sit down and shiver.

The women have to take off their makeup and wear a "Shana Madela", which is usually a wig, great for hiding gray and thinning hair. Men are supposed to make a tear in their clothing and wrap a plain piece of cloth around their bodies to show their grief. This works out well because it's a good excuse to cut-up their old, soiled underwear so they get a little more use out of it.

Another way to defy gravity is to just put an egg-white mask on your skin so your face doesn't move. It's a little difficult to eat or drink or smile, but anything for the sake of not looking older. Buy a carton of eighteen eggs and you can fry some of them for breakfast before they hit their expiration date (or your expiration date), whichever comes first.

Once we have worn our soft lambskin face for many years it starts looking more like an alligator with a home tanning machine. Our once moist, pliable skin begins to sag, and these delightful wrinkles start appearing. Our rear ends start to disappear and then they run away from home. I think they get reincarnated into some twenty-year-olds cute derriere. They never come back home. We have to file a missing butt report.

Some of us start getting bags under our eyes that look like little change purses, or sunken eyes with dark circles that look like we will never sleep. Our noses get bigger, our lips get smaller, and our chins disappear. Our necks start looking like an expandable garden hose. Our teeth start getting yellow and we have to have them to have them bleached so white they blind people when we smile. The good news is that our laugh lines get deeper, a sign that we've been laughing our way through this whole aging process, or just haven't been using a good face cream.

Now that we've survived the pandemic and know how to deal with all the potential Covid variants, we can wear a face mask all the time to cover up those deep upper-lip wrinkles and marionette lines around our mouths and chins unless we need to eat. I solved the problem, I just cut a big hole in my face mask. Maybe it's a good way to have safe sex too.

Then there is the memory of our sexy younger legs. Now the varicose veins are starting to pop like a satellite map. I tried following the map and ended up at my feet, which turned out to be a mangled mess of hammer toes, callouses, and corns. We see ads on TV showing how to use special razors for shaving our pubic hair and deodorant soap made just to keep our crotches smelling good for ten days. Who lets their crotches rot for ten days? Next, there will be nude people having sex on commercials for condoms showing us how strong their condoms are. I yearn for the old commercials showing Texaco men in white jumpsuits putting gas in our cars for us. Now the only commercial for gas is for Gas-X, which we older people really need because everything we eat as we get older gives us gas.

Our waists expand and our clothes don't fit us anymore. I think this is a conspiracy between God, clothing companies, and fast-food chains in order to make us buy new clothes and belts every year. Once our waists expand and we're too old to be pregnant, we have a choice of wearing our pants backward so that our stomach is where our rear ends used to be or buying bigger clothing. (I think there's a possibility that people could get so heavy that Earth could fall out of the Universe.) And why are the airlines making their seats smaller and smaller if people are getting bigger and bigger? Do they have to buy a separate seat for each buttock? *"Will the buttock in seat 12A come to the front of the plane please?"*

We spend our lives going to dermatologists to assure us that our unsightly crusty brown spots aren't melanoma, but just crusty old brown age spots. We get Botox shots and filler to fill in the deep wrinkles, only to find out that we've put a thousand-dollar dermatology bill on a 29.99% interest credit card and the wrinkles come right back four weeks later before we've even paid our credit card bill off. (Why do they have to make the 29.99%. Can't they be honest and say 30%?)

I've decided to go *au naturelle* because I like having enough money to eat and having a roof over my head, even if it's in Las Vegas now, which is either way too hot or way too cold to go out and there's no place to go anyway. No one ever sees me anyway except doctors, and that's only when they run in and out of the little fluorescent cubicle in thirty seconds flat.

As we get older, we get a little more paranoid. I am positive that someone is looking at me through my smartphone or TV or iPad. Last week I was wearing a tank top around the house because it was so hot. Immediately I kept on getting a lot of ads for creams that get rid of sagging, crêpey arms. (Crisco would do the same thing. A jar of it is $5.18 at Walmart and we could have enough left over to bake a few pies.) How would Google know that if they hadn't seen my bare arms, which I always keep covered like all of my aging female friends? Men don't care, they just wear a tank top, Bermuda shorts, and sandals with socks and call it a day. They don't even care about their varicose veins. They think their leg hair covers everything. Hah! We women can see your scrawny hairless legs.

Liver spots start appearing on our arms and legs. I don't know why they call them liver spots. I never ate liver, or even chopped liver or Pâté. My liver is probably the only organ I have that still works perfectly. There's only one thing that works, and that's having a dermatologist freeze off these little brown buggers. I tried and it worked, but now the spots are white, and it looks like I have vitiligo. I would try skin bleach to even out my arms, but I just Googled it and found an article from Medical News Today that said that skin bleaching creams are toxic to humans and contain mercury, which is a heavy toxic metal that will cause numbness, tingling, and muscle convulsions in your legs and give you coordination issues, another name for clumsiness, which I already have anyway.

I read on the Internet that sunscreens are toxic and contain harmful chemicals that affect your hormones and harm fetuses, not that I was planning on getting pregnant anytime soon, but just to be on the safe side, I always wear long sleeves and just sweat, ignoring my body odor because I also read on the Internet that deodorants are toxic because they contain aluminum and cause confusion and muscle weakness, which I already have too. The good news is that as you age, you don't sweat as much and don't have much body odor, unless you're in menopause and have night sweats for eleven years. I started getting ads on Facebook for the lines on my upper lip from years of smoking and drinking from straws and I realized the Internet snoopers were looking at my face too, so I started wearing paper bags over my head. Now I'm getting ads for paper bags in bulk.

Hair Loss. Thinning hair is a problem for all sexes. When people get older and start losing hair, they get more religious. The men start wearing yarmulkes, skullcaps, Kufis, or whatever. The jocks like to wear baseball caps, so they look hip. Some men like to wear their baseball caps in reverse. This way we women won't notice the seborrheic keratosis on their foreheads. We women just think it's stupid. Why don't you men just walk backward?

Other men massage Rogaine in their hair and wear toupees or actual male wigs that usually look like a bird's nest landed on their heads. Others have hair transplants, which make their heads look like freshly planted alfalfa sprouts. Others try to fool you with a comb-over that makes them look like Adolph Hitler, while others shave their heads altogether and grow a full mustache and beard. If they stand on their heads, they actually look like they grew a full head of hair, it's just in the wrong place. I yearn for a pair of scissors when I see these men with really long beards.

Women lose hair as they age too. The sides thin out first, then the top of their heads, magically reappearing as thick, wiry black chin hair that they have to pluck out every day. They're sentenced to a life of tweezing and wearing cute wigs and hats. This is actually a makes it easier for women to hide their flaws. We're getting a reward for having to bear the pain of childbirth. Men have to endure the pain of hair transplants and the embarrassment of having their toupees blown off in a hurricane. Hah! We got even.

I have to face it; I'm getting to be an old jalopy and I'm trying to restore myself with aftermarket parts so

I can become an expensive classic car. The problem is that once I start pulling off the old worn-out parts and replacing them with non-original parts the value goes down and the cheap paint job starts cracking and peeling and drying up like an old crocodile bag that no one wants, even the Goodwill store. *Aha! That's why they call aging women old bags!*

As I've gotten older, I say "Honey" and "Sweetie" and "Dear" a lot because I can't seem to remember anyone's name anymore unless they're wearing a name tag, and even then, I have to put on my glasses to read their name tag. It's really hard for my husband and our dog to wear name tags around the house, especially Lulu, our little dog, because I can't pin it to her skin, so I always call them Sweetie or Honey. They don't know the difference, especially my husband, who can't hear without his hearing aids anyway. I like to call Lou nasty names when he has his hearing aids off just to be funny. I hope he doesn't learn how to read lips. Here's how our conversations go:

"Honey, do you want some prune juice," I asked him nicely.

"I can't hear you!" he screams.

"Do you want your prune juice now!" I shout back at him.

"I don't like your tone of voice! You've got a bad attitude!" he yells back at me.

"I'm not screaming at you. You don't have your hearing aids in, so you can't hear me,"

I say nicely, gritting my teeth with loving frustration.

"What did you say?" he asks.

"I shout, "Do you want some f--king prune juice!!!"

"Don't tell me what to do!" he screams. "You're always degrading me!"

I give up trying to communicate and walk out of the room to give myself a pedicure, but the nail polish I meticulously put on my toenails bleeds down onto my hammer toes and glues them together so I can't wear my sandals in 110-degree weather. I still refuse to spend money on a professional pedicure anymore.

Last time I walked into a nail salon I asked the manicurist, "Do you take walk-ins?

"Why, you no have car?" the manicurist asks.

"My car won't fit through your door," I tell her.

"What you want?" she asks.

"A mani/pedi" I tell her. "How much does that cost?"

"Sixteen dollars," she says.

"Okay, I say" as I climb up into the pedicure chair trying not to show the pain of the metal rod through my tibia, a knee replacement, and hundreds of staples in my chest that all make me a little clumsy. (I've got so much hardware in my body that I could be sold for scrap metal when I die. Who knows? Maybe even when I'm still alive.) I'm exhausted and feel like I've just climbed Mount Everest by the time I figured out how to sit in the spa chair, so I put my aching feet in the boiling water and feel like my feet are lobsters being boiled alive.

"Your feet are velly bad," she says to me lifting one bright red foot out of the boiling water.

"Well, I'm velly old, they match," I say.

I just want to relax, so I lean back and press a button on the massaging chair, and I feel these wood rolling pins pounding quickly on my back as if it's tenderizing filets of beef for stroganoff. If I wanted to get beat up, I would have gone to South Central L.A.

When she's done, she hands me a bill for $80.

"I thought it was only $60?" I ask.

"Your feet velly bad, velly bad," she says.

"Your manicure is velly bad too," I say as I hand her a credit card and sign the bill for the $80, no tip.

"*Wha? No tip!?* You supposed to tip me twenty percent in America!" she screams at me.

"Tips are for good service only in America. They're not required. You lied about the price and added $20 extra," I explained. "You're up $4 on the deal. It's a higher percentage than you can make in the stock market these days."

She gets up and wheels me over to the front of the nail salon in the chair I was sitting in and shoves me and my hands and feet under this fluorescent light, ruining my mani/pedi and making the blue veins in my hands and feet look like I had already died and run over by a tractor.

As a happiness coach and a survivor of life, I've learned to laugh at life, myself, and how I look as I age. It is what is. If we want to age happily and feel young, we need to do whatever we can to look and feel our best, go with the flow, and find humor in every situation.

CHAPTER THREE
Is Your Mirror Lying?

O MG, WHO'S THAT in the Mirror? It's the shock of your lifetime; the day of reckoning. You walk past your bathroom mirror, and you see your father, or mother, or worse, Uncle Boris, the mortician. You close your eyes and open them again, hoping that you're hallucinating or having a bad dream. What are they doing in my mirror? Is this a trick? *What the hell happened?* Did David Copperfield move in? (Well, he's kind of cute. Maybe he wants to have sex with me? He can use it in his Vegas act and make his penis disappear.) Nope, it's you.

Call the aging police! How did I get this old? Where did that little girl with buck teeth, frizzy hair, and big feet go? I think she's locked inside the dyed blonde hair, boob job, and Spandex pants. *No! No! I'm still here!* See, my frizzy hair is straightened thanks to my hair straightening iron, my chin has receded, my teeth are buck again because my parents used a cheap orthodontist, and my big feet are even bigger. I'm still young. Help! Please get me out of this old body!

Remember that day you were getting ready to go out to a nice restaurant or event and looked in the mirror and said to yourself, *I really look good, but this might be the last day I look this great.* Or when you were very young and couldn't wait until you got older? Well, be careful what you wish for, you might just get it.

You move closer to the mirror and see crepe paper worry lines etched on the bridge of your nose. Your nose has gotten a little bigger. Your mouth and lips have gotten thinner. Your jowls look like they're storing a couple of walnuts for dinner, and your chin, *well, er,* chins, are so big that you can't see your neck, which is a good thing because that doesn't look so good either. Your beautiful shiny locks have gotten a little dull and thinner and there's a little gray hair growing in like weeds. And "OMG, where have your thick eyebrows gone?"

You look down at your body and your waist has expanded and your thighs and rear end look like an elephant's ass. Your boobs are pointing to hell, or your penis and balls have gotten longer. What is going on? The Bandit of Youth has attacked. This is a war baby! Let's arm ourselves with wigs and toupees and vials of Botox and fillers and kill and fight like hell against this wicked intruder that is trying to steal our youthfulness.

I wasn't going to give in to aging. Was I being punished for stealing that comic book when I was five years old? It's time to act and max out our credit cards! I didn't know where to start at first. It was like rebuilding the Sistine Chapel. It made me realize that no matter how old you are, everyone still wants to still look handsome or pretty, or is it just me? The day you give in to being old is the day you stop laughing. So, let's pull ourselves together and have fun no matter what our age, which, to be honest, is not just a number, it's a damn wake-up call.

Our girlfriends used to talk about going out to dinner and big events or the latest trends in makeup and clothes or going to Chippendales to watch grown men making idiots of themselves. Our husbands or boyfriends were ogling young girls in miniskirts and big breasts and bragging about their Ferraris and big erections. (They were hiding their Viagra and Cialis in the back of their underwear drawer.) Life was fun and we were carefree, well sort of. I had our two difficult daughters and my mother, my aunt, and my husband's father whom all had dementia to take care of, my businesses to run, our house to take care of, and stepping over bums in Palisades Park, and fighting Los Angeles traffic. Other than that, it was easy, at least up to then.

Time flies by fast; now you're young, *poof*, now you're old. It happens overnight. There wasn't any time in between to adjust. All of a sudden, our friends only wanted to talk about constipation, laxatives, toilet habits, organic food, vitamins, Tai chi, yoga, and going out to a TEDx lecture about stool softeners.

"My bowel movements are so big and hard they look like brown golf balls," one girlfriend says.

"Mine look like matzo balls floating on top of Lake Mead," another friend gloats. (I didn't have the heart to tell her that it was the gas in her stools that made them float and besides, there's a drought and there's hardly any water left in Lake Mead to float in. There's only old rusty barrels with dead gangsters stuffed in them.)

As we grow older, we shrink, so it should be called "shrink older". My husband used to be 6'1" tall and now he's 5"10" which works out great because I can't wear 3" high heels anymore because I fall over. We talk every day to each other about our aches and pains. I woke up this morning with so many aches and pains that I felt like an old creaky house that is settling, settling for what I don't know, an aging life, I guess. It's better than the alternative, being dead, at least I think so. I asked a few dead people this question, but they didn't answer me.

We also talk about our doctors' visits, arthritis, cholesterol, blood pressure, heart rate, memory loss, cataracts, and herniated discs, along with what bargains we got at Costco and the newest anti-aging skin creams, none of which work. We trade advice about vitamins and minerals for our myriad diseases and conditions, our diets, and how to cure our constipation with more fiber and lemon juice (which also works for bleaching out our liver spots), what not to eat for our IBS, and how we are drinking apple cider vinegar to cure all our conditions as well as clean our windows and kill the mold in our shower stalls. We compare manicurists and their fees and bad attitudes, our hairdressers who charge too much, and the vacations we want to take when it's safe, which will never be unless we decide to age happily in spite of all the news, we hear on cable news.

I've even renamed our centuries. BC now means *Before Covid* and AC means *After Covid*. The new variants keep on popping up like little brown spots on our arms. Remember Monkey Pox? We all started hating monkeys. It seems like everyone wants some group to hate. They are joining cults on the Internet in order to make new friends, like the Well-Hung Warriors. Women don't like to brag about their vaginas. One is uglier than the next. I can't figure out why men like them so much, but *whatever*. Or why someone would want to become a gynecologist and look at those things all day?

I think I'm going to start my own group, call it Worn-Out Women. We can organize insurrections at all the nursing homes and try to overturn the kitchen staff and unite to abolish Jell-O. Lou wants to start a group for grumpy old men, Toilet Warriors, they can gang up to overturn their mates to allow them to sit on the toilet all day when they're not taking naps or playing golf. I don't understand why men like golf, you hit a ball into a hole with a stick, big deal. Try putting nail polish on your hammer toes that you got from wearing pointed high-heeled shoes you used to attract men, now that's a real challenge.

I've started taking my blood pressure and temperature all day when I'm home. It gives me something to do other than eat ice cream, do the laundry, watch cable news, check my emails (I don't even get hate mail) and scroll through my text messages, usually from my pharmacy telling me my prescription is ready or asking me to fill out a review of every product I've ever bought on Amazon and every chat agent whose accent I couldn't understand. Then I scroll through invitations and notifications on Facebook and Linked In (at least I still get invited to something), and then start writing. Lulu, my eleven-pound cockapoo, stares at me all day as if she's saying, *"Get a Life, but just keep throwing that ball for me to run after all day."* She ought to analyze the purpose of her own life.

This is an upside-down illogical world we live in now. The new normal is *no* normal. It's like living life standing on your head. As we age, it gets harder and harder to accept that logic no longer exists and that we live in a world that no longer makes sense. I can't figure anything out anymore. We have to use reverse logic in our minds if we want to understand things. For instance, in the stock market; when a company announces that it's going to go into bankruptcy, the stock goes up 50% that day. If it announces stellar earnings, the stock goes down 50% on the same day. "Killing it" and "Crushing it" now means that you did great. "Shredding it" means getting ripped while getting ripped now means paying too much for something. Is a pineapple upside-down cake now a right-side-up cake? *Go figure.* There are shows like "Hookers on Ice." Shouldn't they be on beds? Or nuns on roller skates. Shouldn't they be in a convent or helping poor people? Why do they keep on reducing the number of air controllers while increasing the number of airline flights. Don't they notice that the planes are almost flying into each other every day? And the coup d'état, why don't we keep daylight savings time all year if we're in an energy crisis?

Right is wrong. Wrong is right. Making an "okay" sign with your fingers is now a white supremacy sign. Compliment a woman about her new hairdo and you might have to pay a multi-million-dollar sexual harassment settlement. If a woman asks you, "How do you like my new sweater?" You have to plead the Fifth Amendment.

As we get older people treat us as if we're stupid or senile. They refer to older people as "nice little old lady" or "nice little old man." What do they call old people who aren't "little"? How come people think that if you're old you're really nice? There are plenty of mean, nasty older people. Why does everyone talk nicely about you after you die when you know they were talking badly about you behind your back while you're still alive? Wouldn't it be better to say nice things about you while you were still alive? Does anyone say bad things about you at your funeral? Could everyone that died have been so wonderful?

Aging can really suck if you don't find the

humor in it. It is our *attitude* about aging that can make us crumble like an old stale piece of cornbread or blossom like a beautiful flower. In order to stay young and age happily forever, we need to learn from all of our experiences and use each day to become a better human being and be able to say at the end, "I've really enjoyed the gift of life and have made the world a better place in some small way". We need to accept that we are not the best human beings in the world, nor are we the worst, but we are the best we can be right now.

Aging happily and staying youthful is a work in progress. We learn to accept our limitations, cherish ourselves, use our unique talents, be grateful for the friends and family we still have left (even if it's only your dog, cat, or goldfish), and have enjoyed the life that we were meant to live, not the life anyone else has told us or implied that we should live.

We can finally not feel guilty for doing what we really want to do and enjoy every day we have left. We are free to turn off our TVs, Internet, smartphones and ignore the insurrections, pandemics, droughts, hurricanes, tornados, floods, earthquakes, opioid epidemic, and mass shootings. We all know the world is a mess now and maybe it will heal itself someday, but we're realistic enough that there are only a few little things that we can do to make it better. Let's finally let go of the pandemic, the social unrest, the wars, our enemies, climate change, and whatever it is we need to let go of, and start really enjoying the years we have left, no matter what our age. Let's remember to look at and appreciate what is good in our lives and stop complaining about what is bad in our lives. This is how we age gracefully.

Okay, so life hasn't exactly turned out how you had hoped it would, mine didn't, and maybe you are bitter and angry. Or maybe it has turned out how you wanted it to and you're still unhappy. People live their lives as facades, as the way they think others want to see them. All of your Facebook friends aren't always happy even though they post pictures of themselves enjoying great parties, dinners, and big family events. Everyone hurts inside sometimes, just like us. Maybe you've hit a point in life when you've lived well, enjoyed life, traveled, have good friends, a good mate, and yet you still feel empty. You are depressed and feeling like you want to cry. What is that? It is a feeling of having no real purpose!

Purpose is the fuel that will help us find laughter and happiness as we age. This means accepting who and what you are, and what you can and cannot achieve. *Your purpose must match your reality.*

As a happiness coach, I believe that the meaning of my life is to share with anyone who will listen to my experiences and humor about aging and staying young, to feel the pain with me, to feel the love I want us all to have, whether we're male or female, or "other", or whatever race or religion we are, or whether we're still young or thinking about our golden years. Let's change any negativity or unhappiness we have or had in our lives into joy, gratitude, and humor. Life and aging can be fun if we try to find the humor in almost everything. A positive attitude is the magnet that attracts good luck, success, youthfulness, and joy. If you find the meaning of *your life*, you will find the secret to happiness forever.

What you focus on is what you will get, so let's focus on laughing as we all age in sync. Laughing is what keeps us young! So, we didn't get to travel all over the world, and we didn't end up rich, maybe even ended up alone. What *is* important and gives us pleasure is that we have learned to enjoy each day doing the things we love to do and hope that we will still be able to do them until the day we just go to sleep and don't wake up again. It could be tomorrow or many years away. This is why we should think and act young. *Laughing is the best pain killer and has no side effects other than laugh lines.*

CHAPTER FOUR
Games People Play

THE TEMPERATURE GAME. This is when you're both at home and you feel hot (not the horny type of hot), so your mate insists they are cold. You sneak over to the thermostat and turn up the air conditioning. When your mate realizes you've turned up the air conditioning, they sneak over to the thermostat and turn on the heat. This goes on all day and night until your mate finally falls asleep. Snoring signifies you are the winner.

The Gaslighting Game. You innocently say to your mate, "Look at the sky, honey, it's so blue today."

"No, it isn't. "You're imagining it. The sky looks red" your mate insists.

This is a trendy game for people who love to drive their mates crazy, and usually ends with breaking up or a divorce.

One time Lou and I were going on a trip to Canada

and the only seats left on our flight were the two back seats, right in front of the bathrooms with seat backs that don't recline. They always put older people in the back of the plane on purpose. *You're old, what does it matter if you get sucked out of the back door of the plane.* The jet engines revved up and the plane is ready to take off any second, but just as the wheels are lifting off the runway, I look behind me. The back door of the plane is unlocked and slightly open.

"Honey, the back door of our plane is open!" I scream.

"Don't be ridiculous!" he replies. "You always think negatively. The pilots have a light in the cockpit that tells them if a door was open," he says, trying to make me wrong.

The plane is off the ground now and gaining altitude fast.

"Listen, you stubborn bastard, I'm telling you the back door of this plane is open," I screamed louder.

He looks at me as if I was insane as I wave my hands frantically at several flight attendants who are busy complimenting each other's hairstyles.

"The back door is open!" I scream at them.

They look at me as if I'm interrupting their very important conversation now about whether or not to get Botox injections.

We're going faster and faster and I scream louder and point frantically to the back of the plane pointing at the open door. Four flight attendants finally panicked as all of them run to the back of the plane and force the door closed with their bodies and lock the door mid-flight.

"We almost got just sucked out of the plane," I said to Lou.

"You always take things too seriously," he tells me and adds "and you worry too much."

I was being gaslighted.

Patronizing Game. In this game, you take your mate with you to buy some new clothes and you try on these cute pants because you think they really flatter the junk in your trunk.

"Should I buy these pants honey?" you ask.

"Everything always looks perfect on you honey," your mate says, wanting to hurry you up so they can get back home to watch the football game, and you feel very flattered even though you must admit your rear end looks like the back of the cement mixer truck. The next week you're going out to dinner with your mate and another couple, the Finkelstein's, and you've just got time to change, so you put on the cute pants your mate seemed to think you looked perfect in last week when you bought them, and you ask them, "How do I look?"

"Do you have to wear those horrible pants?" your mate asks. "They make your butt look like the back of an elephant and the Finkelstein's are hunters." You give up and never take your mate shopping with you again.

Guilt-Giving Game. This game goes something like this: "You left the freezer door open last night honey," you tell your mate, trying to sound nice.

"You're always criticizing me," your mate replies as if you've turned their ego into instant mashed potatoes.

"All the meat and chocolate ice cream are dripping all over the floor honey and it looks like a crime scene," you explain.

"You don't think I can do anything right!" your mate says accusingly.

They might be right. "You do a lot of things right honey. This is just one thing. It's not an assault on your entire being," you explain.

"All you had to do was clean it up," your mate screams at you.

Your mate won. You clean it all up.

Another guilt-giving technique goes something like this: You buy some of your favorite cookies and put them out on the kitchen counter. "Hi honey, I got *us* some of *our* favorite chocolate chip cookies," you announce.

"Thank you. That was very sweet of you, sweetie," your mate replies.

The next day you look on the kitchen counter and the cookies are all gone. You were dying to eat some of those cookies, but your mate ate them all. You are seething. "Where did you put the chocolate chip cookies, sweetie? you ask nicely with gritted teeth.

"Oh, I ate them all. I thought you said they were all for me," your mate says sheepishly.

"I was dying to eat some!". You want to kill you mate, but you don't want to go to prison. Anyway, none of the kitchen knives are sharp enough anymore.

"I'm sorry, I must have heard you wrong," your mate says guiltily, blaming it on his hearing.

"That's okay Honey, you work hard…*spending your life laying on the bed watching TV.* I think there's a box of some old stale dried-out Fig Newtons with bugs in it in the back of the pantry I can force myself to eat."

Embarrassing Your Children Game. This is an old-time game that I learned from my parents. My mother liked to play this game whenever I was in the back seat and my father wanted to change lanes. She would roll down her window, stick her whole body out the window, and wave her arms like one of those inflatable tube men in front of carpet stores.

"Yoo-hoo, Mister!" She would scream out the window as if the person in the other car could hear her.

I would duck down in the back seat so no one would see me with them. When you're young you really care what other people think of you. As you age, you don't care as much because you have figured out that everyone is only thinking about themselves.

Lou once signed a three-year lease for a bright metallic turquoise Corvette without asking me. It was so ugly that no one at any car dealership would buy it, so he wanted to surprise me with his new car. *I was surprised.* I spent three years ducking down in the passenger praying no one would see me. (Okay, I'm human. I still kind of care what others think.)

The Back Seat Driving Game. This is one of the best games to get your mate to stop talking to you for a day or two when you need some quiet time. When Lou is riding another car's tail, I scream at him "Back off. You're not leaving enough room to stop!"

"I don't want anyone to sneak in front of me!" he argues.

"Sweetie, if you are going 65 miles an hour and another car cuts in front of you going 65 miles per hour, you are going to get to your destination at the exact same time, less the length of one car, about ten feet, or one second later. So, you have a 99.99% chance of making it to your destination on time. But if the car in front of you stops suddenly and you're tailgating, you have a 99.99% chance of hitting it," I explain. *Sounds logical.*

"I don't care, I don't want anyone to sneak in front of me!" he screams stubbornly as if the car is some A-hole kid cutting in front of him in the school cafeteria line because it's Italian surprise day. *I choose to be happy, so I close my eyes and pray for the best.*

Next, he's going through this roundabout that some power-hungry politician in our local government decided to build to piss off drivers in our neighborhood. There's a sign marked.

"Yield" as you enter the roundabout. Every time we go through a roundabout, I put my head down and close my eyes and say a Hail Mary even though I'm not Catholic. *Of course, when I'm driving it's a different story.*

Googling for Gout Game. This is one of my favorite games. You put all your symptoms in the search bar and see how many diseases you can find that match your ailments. So far, I've come up with 10,000. Of that, there are 5,000 I think I have. So, when I can't sleep at night, I fire up my smartphone or tablet and see if I can find more.

Googling for Side Effects Game. This is when you Google every prescription and OTC drug you've ever been prescribed and bring up the side effects. There are about 5000 known side effects, so if you do the math, you will always find that the prescription medications are causing more symptoms than the symptoms of the disease you're trying to cure.

When I have insomnia, I watch TV and all the ads for new prescription drugs. I can't figure out why they make drugs for constipation, diarrhea, rash, eczema, high blood pressure, low blood pressure, hair loss, dizziness, nausea, and vertigo when the side effects of the drug are exactly the same and *could also cause death*. Why would you take that medication and risk death? *Corporate profits? Ya think?*

Is everyone on drugs? Why do they still build houses with medicine cabinets in bathrooms when all medicines say, "do not store in the bathroom?" It's as ridiculous as putting warning signs on pillows and mattresses that say, "It is a Federal Offense to remove this tag!" Is anyone stupid enough to believe that the FBI is going to come to their house to arrest them for tearing off a warning tag? *Yes, I've never removed one warning tag.*

Once my pains got so bad that I bought some of those lidocaine pads and plastered them all over my body, except my vagina, nose, mouth, and ears, which were the only parts of my body that were visible. The problem was I couldn't get them off of me for a week. I've gone off all prescriptions and now I feel great except for my arthritis, herniated disk, trigger finger, gastritis, ulcers, a rod through my tibia, and a knee replacement. Other than that, I'm like a nineteen-year-old.

Knee replacements are great. My surgeon sent me over this machine that you lie in bed and press up and down with your leg all day, so I put some grapes on it and made some Chianti. Then the medical insurance company sent over this woman to give me a shower, but the only person I'd let give me a shower is George Clooney. Then they sent over a physical therapist, and he gave me this little machine with pedals that you put on the floor, then told me to sit in a chair and pedal all day. Why don't hamsters get bored?

I have so many diseases and conditions I can't even figure out what I can eat without going into anaphylaxis. I once went to a dietician to have her figure out for me what I could actually eat, and she handed me some printouts from the Internet and a coupon for Ensure. Apparently, the only thing I was allowed to eat was kale with Ensure. So, I decided to throw caution to the wind and take a Ouija board with me to the market and restaurants. Whatever it tells me to eat, I eat. *F--k it all.* This is how you stay young and happy forever!

CHAPTER FIVE
How To Stop Being Invisible

IT WAS THE day I moved to Las Vegas and woke up the next morning, looked in the mirror, and nothing was there. *Nada.* I didn't exist. I blamed it on the dry desert heat, trick mirrors, bad lighting, or anything I could blame it on other than admitting that I was aging, and older people become invisible. I bought a giant bottle of dark tanning cream and slathered it all over my face and body, but this just stained all my clothes. I could see my stained clothes in the mirror, but not myself. *Could anyone else see me?*

I stopped using crosswalks for fear I would get hit by a car, but being invisible was good for sneaking into movie theaters. One time this big fat guy sat on top of me, of course not knowing I was sitting there. I had to watch a two-hour movie with this guy in my lap. The gig was over. No more sneaking into movie theaters.

I was walking past a nice-looking older man, and he smiled at me. I was very flattered and smiled back at him. He didn't smile back. I guess I was still invisible. I turned my head and realized that he had been looking right through me at this sexy twenty-year-old blonde behind me with Grand Canyon cleavage. She smiled back at him. I didn't like being invisible, so I fixed him and called to him loudly, "Come on daddy, you're lost again. I'll take you back to mommy."

As I get older, everyone looks younger than me. Doctors start looking like they just got out of kindergarten. They probably got their medical degree from an ad for some online medical school that they found in an airline magazine. I went to this new doctor, waited an hour shivering in an over-air-conditioned waiting room and watching re-runs of Property Brothers, another hour sitting on an exam table covered with white butcher paper in a tiny cubicle room flooded with fluorescent lights that illuminate every flaw on my naked body while trying to change positions in a flimsy paper gown that kept on ripping apart.

Finally, this pubescent doctor finally skateboards into the room, introduces himself as Dr. Billy and asks, "How are *we* doing?" as if he really cares.

What's this "we" s**t? "You might be doing fine but I'm invisible and this fat man sat on me and crushed my ribs, but other than that I'm doing great."

Dr. Billy writes something in his coloring book. "I'm so glad you're doing better," he replies. *Maybe he is losing his hearing too, so I give him the benefit of the doubt.*

"Let me see you again in two weeks. I'll send a prescription to your pharmacy," he says as he scribbles on his prescription pad with his crayon.

A prescription for what? Aging? I'm still invisible. I could walk around naked, no one would notice. Younger people think we're almost dead, and dead people don't need doctors, they need caskets. Maybe doctors want a kickback along with the ones from the insurance and pharmaceutical companies. Why not get a kickback from mortuaries too?

I go over to my pharmacy to pick up the magic prescription that will cure my aging and make me visible again, which is probably an aspirin with a pretty pink coating on it. The girl at the pharmacy with the long rhinestone-embedded blue talons and long false eyelashes, doesn't give a s--t about me. She hands me an RX bottle and glares at me with an *attitude*, "That will be a $5000 copay," she tells me, as if using my life savings for a prescription that is useless is no big deal.

As we get older, we like to fill up our social calendars, more commonly known to us older people as Dates with Doctors. I like to fill up every square with at least one appointment a day to feel popular, so I make appointments with urologists, gynecologists, cardiologists, gastroenterologists, ENTs, or anyone that has the courage to look into my orifices or can tell me that I look good for my age. I called some girlfriends to have some lunch. They always tell me how good I look.

There are a lot of fun things to do as you age, like CT scans, MRIs, ultrasounds, x-rays, mammograms, and whatever new torture machine they can bill to our insurance. I've had so many CT scans that I can light up a Christmas tree and so many MRIs that paper clips stick to me. I used to get my yearly mammograms at this place called The Chamber of Agony. This Russian sadist, Stalin reincarnated, put each of my breasts into this torture machine and lowered these two pieces together so that my breast was completely flattened. I screamed in pain. "Open this thing up. You're killing me!"

"Be patient! I *hov* to get a good *peekture*" she would tell me, as if they were going to use my mammogram in a photo exhibit at the Museum of Ancient History.

"And I have to banish you to a Gulag" I scream as the pain becomes unbearable.

She finally released my breasts, which looked like they just went through the press at Waffle House, and I felt like I was going to faint. All I could think of was maple syrup.

"See, that not hurt at all, did it," she says, careful not to make it a question.

Right, you bitch.

The good news for us aging women is that we don't need to go to the gynecologist anymore because all of our female organs have dried up into pea-size little thingies. The last gynecologist I went to informed me that my ovaries, cervix, and uterus had shrunk to the size of raisins. *Great, now I had the Incredible Shrinking Sex Organs.*

"So, what am I supposed to do, add some nuts, and sprinkle what's left of my sexual organs on top of my cereal?" I asked.

"No, you're getting older," she informed me as if I hadn't noticed.

Maybe they can transplant the sex organs of a twenty-year-old in me like they do livers and hearts. As long as it was female organs, it would be fine. Male organs, not so much. I don't like lumps in my pants. They're worse than panty lines.

Men still have to worry about their penises shrinking and their balls getting longer. You know you've hit rock bottom when your balls hang into the toilet water. The solution to this is to adjust the toilet water so it doesn't fill up so high, which fools your testicles into believing they're younger.

Men also have to worry about their prostate glands and rectal exams. Lou's proctologist waited until he finished the exam to tell him, "You're more likely to die with prostate cancer than die from prostate cancer." So why do doctors have to stick their finger up men's rectums if they're not going to do anything to cure whatever it is they find?" *Do they think they're going to find bars of gold in men's doody holes? Maybe there is gold? Maybe I should look, I love gold jewelry.*

Then there's incontinence. Both women and men get it. Do you know how difficult it is for an older man or woman to "leak" and look everywhere in the drugstore for adult diapers and not be able to find the right aisle? When you're older, you're forced to ask the twenty-year-old stock person, "Do you know where I can find the adult diapers?" The snotty little eighteen-year-old bitch can't stop laughing and points to aisle ten.

You go to aisle ten, find the adult diapers, and coyly sneak them into your shopping cart, covering up the box with a cheap drugstore sweatshirt that you grab from the clothing section. All the shoppers are glaring at you as if you're stealing something, so you're forced to shrug and confess "Okay, so I leak a little!"

Next you go to the long checkout line everyone glares at your cart and chuckles. The sweatshirt has slid off the box of adult diapers. The smartass kid at the cash register starts giggling too. It's not fun getting older, but the good part is that smarty-pants is going to get older someday and he'll find out what it's like. Hah!

When you get home, you put on the cheap drugstore chartreuse sweatshirt because you had to pay for it anyway and it goes so well with the bright red sweatpants you always wear. You look in the mirror and there's a huge picture of some rapper on the front of the sweatshirt. You start singing "Hit Em' Up", grabbing your crotch and jumping up and down just to get your money's worth. You didn't realize your mate was filming you and uploaded it on Tik Tok. It goes viral and you become the newest

Internet sensation. Congratulations! You're finally visible again!

Yesterday I went to a big mall to buy some new underwear because my old underwear was torn. I got so confused about where I had parked my car and wandered around the parking structure until I was sweating and breathing heavily as if I'd just had wild sex. *No such luck.* After an hour of walking around the huge parking structure, I finally found a security guard with an electric cart to help me find my car. He was so nice I wanted to invite him to dinner, but after an hour of the cart ride, I finally remembered that I had taken an Uber.

That night I had insomnia because of a bad rectal itch. I finally fell asleep only to be awakened early by my own sleep apnea. I was worried about the worst-case scenario, having my rectum removed, so I called my doctor, who gave me the name of a good general surgeon. *Maybe he thought I really did need my whole rectum removed? A rectumotomy.*

I called the surgeon, Doctor Tush, and a recording comes on with twenty options, but none of them say "rectal itch." I tried the menu again, thinking that "new patient" was probably right, although I was losing my patience. Another recording comes on that says "Please hold for the next caring team member. You are 25th in line. We value your call." *Yeah, sure. I bet you value my call.*

Ninety minutes later some emotionless robot comes on the phone and tells me "There are no new appointments for three months." My rectal itch is driving me crazy. I can't go anywhere without people thinking I'm a pervert.

"Okay, I'll take the first available," I give in.

I walk around for three months scratching my rear end and the day finally comes. I get showered and dressed nicely just in case Dr. Tush is good-looking, I think I'm visible now and looking good. I sit in the waiting room watching gallstone surgeries on the TV, and then remember I might have put my underwear on backwards, or even worse, forgotten to put them on at all. It didn't matter.

Dr. Tush (who *is* really hot) comes in and says, "Lean over and spread your cheeks."

Did he want to see if I was smuggling drugs? I put my fingers in my mouth and spread my cheeks.

He doesn't laugh. I spread my buttocks.

"It's nothing" he says, handing me a free sample of corticoid cream.

It was degrading. He called my rectum a nothing. I waited three months for an OTC tube of cortisone cream and to have my rectum insulted. Even my rectum was unimportant. I've decided to use *Telehealth* appointments as much as I could. It's much easier and quicker and you get to wear your pajamas and have food stuck in your teeth and keep your dog in your lap while talking to your doctor, who's probably on the toilet. The big problem is when you need a vaginal or rectal exam. It's hard to get your smartphone screen between your legs and you definitely can't fit an iPad unless you're really bow legged.

We needed a new car. *Don't ask what happened to the old one.* So, we went to a Kia dealership to lease a new car. *Don't ask how that went.* (Don't ask anything, it's less stressful.) I learned that you become visible when a salesman can make money off of you. We spent hours in the showroom while they kept on insisting that we pay them more than they had quoted on the phone. They were playing the "Let's Keep These Older People Here Until We Wear the Old Suckers Down" and the "They're Too Hungry to Argue" game. I was so hungry I was going to pass out from low blood sugar before I would give in. So now we have a new car. It has tires and a motor, that's all I know. No CD player. Oh, and we paid double what they had quoted us on the phone.

As we start aging, we need colonoscopies. There is nothing more fun than a colonoscopy and the refreshing feeling you get from swallowing a handful of Dulcolax and then drinking a full pitcher of lemon Gatorade mixed with MiraLAX. The good news is that running to the toilet all night burns a lot of calories and makes your stomach look less bloated. It's great if you're up for an Academy Award and want to look thin, as long as you don't win an Oscar the minute your diarrhea starts. Timing is everything in life.

I recently had a colonoscopy and had twelve polyps removed and when I got up the next morning, I had a fever of 102.5 degrees. I went to the ER, they hooked me up to an IV, gave me a Covid-19 test, put me in a wheelchair, and made me wait six hours in the waiting room. It was the height of the Covid pandemic, and we watched as they wheeled dead bodies covered in sheets past the ER waiting room.

They finally told us that they were taking me to the Covid floor. At this point I was so sick that I didn't care if they stuck me in a casket as long as I could lie down, and it was lined with satin. Once I'm in my room alone (# 1313, not a good omen) I hear a female hacking away in the next room. I get into bed and I'm shivering, so I just get under the covers when a nurse finally comes in to take my vital signs. My temperature was 103.5, so she told me to strip. I wasn't sure if I was in a strip club or hospital at this point. She helps me take off everything, packs me in ice, and leaves the room. I just laid there like a salmon filet in the glass fish display at Albertsons. I envisioned myself being wheeled past the ER waiting room with a stained sheet covering *my* body.

They woke me up as soon as I fell asleep to give me sleeping pills *(makes sense)* and take my vital signs. My fever was down, but I felt like I had just gone three rounds with Mike Tyson. I had to feel my ears to make sure they weren't bitten off. I spent a week in the hospital on IV antibiotics and having every test that they could bill to my insurance company. They would bring me special "healthy" meals so I would get better, like mystery meat smothered in canned gravy, instant mashed potatoes covered with thick gravy, and some kind of secret vegetable from a can, and of course, a bowl of Jell-O for dessert. This was a special diet to make invisible patients even more sick. I suspected the hospital dietician was a dropout from some online school and the cook had been fired from San Quentin.

In the middle of the night, I rolled over in my sleep and my IV pulled out of my arm and blood spurted out all over the walls. The room looked like a crime scene. I pressed the nurse's button, but I think they were all watching porno movies and having an orgy. I got out of bed, blood gushing from my arm, and started running up and down the hospital corridor calling out "Nurse! Nurse!" I sounded like an actress in a B-movie. Blood was all over the hospital floor. I thought I was bleeding out.

Finally, a nurse wakes up and finds me still wandering the halls, sees me covered in blood, and tries to put in another IV but apparently had never put in an IV before. I felt like one of those rubber dummies they use in medical school.

"Just bandage me up and I'll take my antibiotics by mouth thank you!"

"Do you want us to wake you up for your shot pain shot tonight or should we do it while you are sleeping?" she asks.

Who feels pain while they're sleeping, but, whatever.

In the middle of the night, I felt a needle go into my arm. *I was awake, or was I?* There were nurses all around me, laughing together as they rolled my body over as if I was a churro being rolled in powdered sugar, and I heard myself mumble *"What's happening? Where am I? What are you doing to me?"* They all laughed.

I was looking down at my body from above, not knowing what was real and what wasn't. There were beams of light shining into my eyes and the room was spinning. I blacked out and when opened my eyes the room was dark and empty. Maybe they had accidentally given me hallucinogenic. I still don't know if I was alive or dead at that time and never will. I could be a real zombie now for all I know. I do have dark circles under my eyes. Maybe they'll cast me in the sequel to Life of the Living Dead.

Very early the next morning a young nurse and her trainee came in the room, woke me up, and introduced themselves as my nurses for today, looked at my chart, and gave me a pill.

"What pill are you giving me?" I asked, taking the little pill with a sip of water.

"We're not sure what it is," they both admit sheepishly.

Great. I was just poisoned by two nurses who got their licenses by reading "Nursing for Dummies." They were like the female version of Will Farrell and Chris Catan in "Night at the Roxbury." Neither one knew what they were doing. The trainer was even dumber than the trainee and they made a bowling ball seem smart. They insisted I had to have an IV in for my antibiotics this morning, so, not even knowing if I was actually alive, I said "Okay". One of them tried shoving a needle up into my vein,

"Oopsy, I popped a vein" she said as if she was

popping a birthday party balloon. I'm finally visible again as I screamed in pain, the blood was spurting out of my arm again. I've heard of bloodletting, but this was ridiculous; next they'll be using leaches on me. I do know a lot of leaches.

"I'm not really trained yet to put in an IV," the trainer nurse confessed as they ran out of the room together as fast as they could, never to be seen again.

Next thing I know is that I'm lying in the bathroom with a bad case of loosies and puking into the toilet at the same time. Apparently, they had given me the wrong pill. The hospital discharge Nazi walks in and hands me my discharge papers, not caring that I'm on the bathroom floor puking into some toilet that thousands of other patients had used.

"Out we go, honey" she says as she shoves my discharge papers into my hand, pretending not to not to notice that I looked like Mount St. Helens erupting. "Medical insurance won't cover any more days so out you go sweety." *It was a very caring moment.*

The second colonoscopy proved that I was giving birth to polyps like bunnies. In the recovery room a nurse showed me pictures of fourteen more polyps that the first gastroenterologist had been too lazy to remove. Some of them looked like cauliflower, others looked like little florets of broccoli. I could make a vegetable salad if I had a little olive oil, balsamic vinegar, and a little Dijon mustard. The nurse handed me all the color photos to put into my family album. I had always wanted a big family, but I had to settle for an extended family of polyps. I named the first one Polly.

The third colonoscopy went as well as passing gas at a daily Muslim prayer. My blood pressure was 200/195. I awoke in the recovery room and the nurse showed me photos of five more polyps, little cuties. I was out of it for a week. *What the hell did the anesthesiologist give me for my blood pressure?*

We all lose some of our hearing as we get older, it goes along with insomnia and constipation. Lou accumulates so much wax in his ears I've been thinking about opening a candle business.

I couldn't hear out of my right ear when I was lying in bed on my left ear. I just wanted to make sure I didn't have any crystals in my ear because I had been a little dizzy, off balance, and falling. *What's a little falling here and there?* The ear doctor's PA examines my ears and tells me there are no crystals (I was hoping to make some crystal earrings) and gives me a long hearing test, then sticks me a room that was so cold I felt like I was being cryopreserved. I was shivering and my individual fake eyelashes I had paid so much for were turning into icicles.

She shows me the chart with my hearing test results. "Well, you do have some hearing loss, a little in the left ear and a lot in the right ear," she says. *Okay, so I'm getting older and most everyone gets a little hearing loss.*

"You may have a tumor causing the difference in your hearing because usually both ears lose hearing at the same rate. There's a small chance that this is the cause of your hearing loss," the PA explains.

Shocked, I asked, "What do they do to get rid of this tumor?"

"You need an MRI to see if there *is* a tumor in your skull first," she replied.

Sounded reasonable I thought, "but how do they remove the tumor if they find one?"

She drew me a diagram and explained how the surgeon saws off the top of your skull and removes the tumor that way. The first thing I thought about was shaving off my hair. I think I probably have an ugly skull. The second thing I thought about was that scene in Hannibal the Cannibal when Anthony Hopkins had sawed off the top of Ray Liotta's skull and was eating his brain with a spoon. I ran out of there as fast as I could. PS, I did have the MRI and my brain is fine.

I finally realized how to solve this invisibility problem. I bought the biggest, meanest looking pit bull I could find and put a big black halter on him that said, "Service Dog." I named him 'Killer.' I was invisible no more.

CHAPTER SIX
The Perks of Getting Older

Y<small>OU GET A</small> *senior discount from stores that offer senior and veteran's discounts.* You can say f--k you to the cheap stores that won't give you a discount. Now you'll just buy at the generous stores that raise the prices 15% and give you a 10% discount.

You get your toenails clipped for free at the podiatrist. Your insurance pays for it. Don't count on nail polish too. Do podiatrists have foot fetishes?

You get to have an airplane employee take you to your gate in a wheelchair and get the bulkhead seat. Enjoy the ride and don't let them see that you can really walk.

There are a lot of good things about being hard of hearing. You can pretend you don't hear someone if you don't want to talk to them. If they turn off their hearing aids too, you can just stare at each other. Next, if you have hearing aids and you don't like a particular conversation, you can just turn off your hearing aids. And third, if you want to annoy your mate or someone obnoxious, you can blast the sound on the TV or scream as loud as you can into the phone. They will think you're hard of hearing and let you get away with it.

You get to park in handicap parking, and no one says a thing to you, even if you're just faking a limp. If they do say something, consider it a compliment.

Women, you can pee on the toilet seat, and everyone will forgive you because you're older. (Older than what, I'm not sure.) Did you ever try to put one of those flimsy toilet seat covers? No matter what you do, they fall into the toilet before you can sit down fast enough. Even if you're quick enough to sit down before it falls into the water, someone else's pee has soaked through the cover, and you have to walk around all day soaking wet with someone else's pee. If you're using one of those motion detector flush toilets, you finally get the tissue cover to stay on the toilet seat and then you race to sit on down, but the toilet flushes automatically and the toilet seat cover gets sucked down into the sewers of civilization. Did you ever have to use a unisex bathroom in a restaurant? Urinals are disgusting to women. Why do they put ice in urinals? Is someone going to order iced urine?

Men, you can pee on the floor of a men's bathroom, and everyone will forgive you because you're getting older. This can be bad for you if the man before you peed on the floor. Stepping on urine can be sticky.

Peeing on the floor of a *unisex* bathroom or leaving the toilet seat up at home punishable by death. Your mate will ban you from having sex for the rest of your life (if you haven't already been).

You can watch the same movies and TV shows over and over again and each time is the first time. This saves money on streaming subscriptions and helps you fall asleep easier. It can also drive your mate crazy, which can be fun.

You don't have to spend as much time doing your hair because you have none left. Covering up the bald spots is time consuming. Hats can get tricky to wear, especially in a hurricane or if you sleep at a new lover's house. I'm thinking of making decorative fake fur stickies to cover bald patches. I can sell them on Amazon, but the problem may be pulling the Velcro strips off your scalp.

You don't care what other people think anymore. You're convinced they don't think anyway. If this is always true, then why do some of us spend so much time and money trying to look younger?

You can eat anything you want if it doesn't' give you heartburn, indigestion, constipation, diarrhea, or makes you throw up. Go ahead and eat ice cream, cake, cookies, muffins, pizza, spareribs, junk food, fast food, anything. Forget the calories and your arteries, you're going to die anyway.

You rarely have body odor. This is because body order is caused by bacteria on the skin that break down the acids in your sweat. The good news is that bacteria doesn't like to hang out on older people, it wants to hang with the young people with active hormones at the gym. When I'm at the gym working out, I can hear people looking at me and whispering to each other, "Why bother?" Ignore these people, working out keeps you young.

Constipation can be an asset. It saves money on toilet paper. Do you remember when your parents used to display the extra roll of toilet paper in the powder room by covering it with a cute, crocheted toilet paper cozy? Now, everyone sticks a package of eighteen mega-rolls from Costco on the bathroom floor. Is it my imagination, but do people use more toilet paper than they used to? Is that why there's always a shortage of it? Have they gone butt crazy?

You can take off your clothes and go wander around naked outside anytime without getting arrested. Everyone will assume you just have dementia and don't know what you're doing. *Just one question, what are you doing?*

Medicare is great. You now have a lot of your medical expenses covered by the US government. The problem is that the doctors who take Medicare treat you like a second-class citizen because Medicare pays them so little for treating you. If you're rich, you can pay a fortune for a concierge doctor, but that's not most of us.

Intuition becomes stronger as we age and becomes the best tool we have to guide us through a happier, safer life as we age. Small red flags become great big red waving flags. We are smart enough to pay attention to these red flags now.

(The rest of this page was left intentionally blank. I can't think of any other perks.)

CHAPTER SEVEN
The Many Shades of Toxic People

ONE OF THE most positive things about aging is that we develop a talent for quickly spotting nutcases and neurotics. We can now recognize good and evil as easily as we can sort out colors in our laundry (unless we're color-blind or male). Our BS antennas grow longer, like our noses, and we can spot who's on our team and who's not quickly. We can even tell who's on Team Jealous by the look on their faces when we tell them we just inherited a million dollars. Clue: They say "Fabulous! I'm so excited for you!" but their expression says *I hate you! I hope you lose it! Can you give me some?*

As we age, we have less and less time on this planet, so we need to find a way to enjoy the good moments we still have left, do the things we really want to do, not things that we think we should do, or things other people tell us we should do. We need to spend our time with the people we enjoy, not the people that drive us crazy or aren't on our team. Every moment is precious. Toxic people are like anti-freeze slipped into your drinking water. They will suck the life out of your body as you unknowingly slowly drink the poison and get weaker and sicker every moment you spend with them. It is amazing how much lighter and happier you will feel when you get these people out of your life. Headaches, stomach aches, back pain, and depression all start to disappear, you start laughing again and you feel free to be you instead of walking on eggshells. You know a person is toxic when they make you feel unhappy, and you can't wait to get away from them.

The Vampire is someone who sucks all the energy out of you, like draining the gasoline out of your gas tank until you're running on fumes. They talk incessantly about trivial things like how grass grows and tell the same story over and over again about how they won a contest for making the best lanyard at day camp. Try to interject your thoughts into a conversation with The Vampire and they talk right through you as if you're not important, or not even there. A conversation with a Vampire is not a conversation, it's a bodybuilding contest between your ears and their mouth muscles. If you're on the phone with a Vampire and know they're just using your ears, hang up the phone quietly and they'll think you got disconnected. *Hopefully, forever.*

The Two-Faced Gecko is a fair-weather friend

that professes how much they care about you, even how much they love you, but they are never there for you when you need them. They are just using you as a warm body to accompany them to restaurants or events, so they don't have to be seen alone, and as a perk, you get to pay the bill. "My wallet was stolen" or "Why don't you get the check this time?" They want you to go with them on a vacation because it's too lonely to go alone. Then, when you're sitting with them at some bar, they start talking to another person they're attracted to, turning their back to you, leaving you to take out your cell phone and read the weather report and scroll around on some online dating site all night.

The next day you find out you have cancer. You write a text message to tell them. Do you think your "loving" friend texts you back or calls you to see how you're doing or offers to go with you to chemo? Nope. You can bet on it. They're too busy having sex with the person they dumped you for last night.

The Mosquito is the insect that always bites you. They are the ones that also forget their wallets every time you have lunch together. I have a client who has a friend named Betty Biter. One time, my client was talking to Betty Biter as she was having sex with her husband's best friend in her front hallway while using her foot to hold the front door shut because her husband was banging on the door to get in. That should have been a red flag about her character. A year later my client got a call from Betty Biter.

"Hi, how are you?" She asked my client.

"I'm in bed trying to recover from pneumonia," my client told her.

"Oh, I'm sorry," said Betty Biter, quickly hanging up the phone on my client. She never heard back from Betty Biter. Please note, "How are you?" does not always mean "How are you?" Often it can mean "Hi, I called to ask you to do something for me but if you can't do anything for me, I'm hanging up right now."

The Chameleon is a two-faced social-climbing phony that wears all designer clothing, accessories, expensive jewelry, drives an expensive car, eats at extravagant restaurants, only flies first class, and will only sleep in expensive hotels. When you go to their home, the first thing they do is check out what designer you're wearing. F--k them, wear all fakes. They won't know the difference. Once you pass the designer clothes test (or not) they take you on a tour through their expensive home (probably in foreclosure) and the first thing they show you is their walk-in closet, which is decorated with designer clothes, shoes, and bags, all lined up exactly an inch apart as if it is a Gucci store. They make sure you never find out that their high-interest credit cards are maxed to the limit by hiding their mail from the debt collectors in their fake Goddard antique secretary desk.

The Chameleon is lovely to you as long as you live their phoniness with them, but don't expect them to be there if you find yourself losing your money, becoming ill, or really just need a friend. They are fair-weathered friends. When they say they love you it is as meaningless as a Hollywood air kiss that misses your cheek and ends up as thick saliva on your ear. It makes The Chameleon happy to make you feel inferior. They will use you to pad their parties, but drop you like a bag of swap meet jewelry if you're down and out. Chameleons only think of themselves, money, social status, and their closets. Don't ask The Chameleon for any favors or to be there for you when you're down. They'll change their colors really quickly and go into hiding.

The Alligator has a lot of the same traits as the Chameleon, but their *only* goal is to swindle you out of all your money. This fast-talking, well-dressed imposter works the Internet, country clubs, health clubs, nightspots, bars, art exhibits, wine tastings, or wherever they can find wealthy people. The Alligator stalks you like a creature scouring the swamps of Florida for a juicy naïve person to nosh on.

I have a client who lost all his money to *Stanley Swindler*, who was a charismatic character that boasted about how much money he was making with a new investment. He wanted my client to invest in this fabulous "opportunity", which was probably something like making energy out of sawdust. (It was more likely that he would make my client's money into sawdust.) He waved his wrist around so my client couldn't help noticing his Cartier watch and diamond pinkie ring (probably fake). The crocodile shoes and Hermes bags were dead giveaways too. He wined and dined my client and his family at trendy expensive restaurants, paying the tab with the money he just swindled from his last victim. Remember, alligators eat people alive. The Alligator disappeared, along with my client's life savings.

Once you allow The Alligator into your life, they will always screw you (sometimes literally), out of money, and worst-case scenario, out of your life. How many Internet predators have gone on to kill their newest Internet "love victim"? I just Googled it but couldn't find an accurate answer. Probably too many to count.

The Snake will stab you in the back. Give The Snake a copy of your book manuscript to read, and they steal it and try to sell it to a publisher. Leave your mate alone with The Snake, and they will try to steal your mate from you. Loan a snake money for food and housing and they will spend it on a lavish trip or drugs.

My client, Foolish Francine, met a great guy on a dating site. Their relationship evolved and he moved in. One morning she got an email from a Corvette dealership thanking her for her purchase of a brand-new Corvette ZO6. He had stolen her American Express card and bought himself a new car.

The Tapeworm prides themself on getting anything they can get for free or anything from you they can finagle. They are cheapskates and are always looking for a free ride, free meal, free place to live, free car, free parking, free clothing, anything free that they can get their hands on, like free sex.

F--k them. Let them pay a hooker. When they do buy something, they use it for a while and then return it, screaming long and loud until the seller takes it back.

I once had a date with a new guy, Will Wormy, who told me he was taking me out to a nice dinner. *Well, it was kind of like taking me out for dinner.* He came to the door dressed in a nice suit and took me to an expensive hotel. He guided me into a large banquet room loaded with other couples. We were the only non-Asians in the room.

Puzzled, I asked, "What is this event?"

"I don't know, some Chinese convention," he said nonchalantly.

Apparently, his mode of operation was to find big corporate dinner events in some newspaper (maybe he read Chinese) and crash them for free meals. I was starving, so I went along with this charade. We walked to a table with two empty chairs, and I bowed to everyone sitting there. *Okay, so I didn't know that Chinese people don't bow, Japanese people, do. Everyone makes mistakes.* I sat down at this table with all the Chinese people clapping for the speaker who was speaking Mandarin, I think. I clapped along with everyone when they clapped for the speaker, praying that the rightful owners of our seats wouldn't show up. The Tapeworm is usually harmless as long as you don't mind a penny-pincher living off of you like a parasite. I personally don't like to feel used.

The Mooch is a serial finagler. Mary Tightwallet and I were close enough to meet for lunch once a week at IHOP. Like clockwork, the check would come, and Mary would open her wallet and say, "I only have one dollar." Her share of the bill was always $1.50 (Yes, in those days that's all an IHOP lunch cost.) I was a sucker and would pay the extra fifty cents every time. Years later when I was married to Lou, I ran into her, and we became friendly again until we went to visit her in her new condo. She mooched a full weekend making us treat her to the most expensive restaurants in Southern California and then acted as if we hadn't done enough for her.

The Guilt Giver is a manipulator with a very strong demanding personality. Their main goal is to control you in order to get what they want from you. Guilt-giving is their specialty, but they'll use extortion if necessary. They'll even look at you with puppy dog eyes. If they still can't get what they want from you, they will move on. Help them pack and load the moving truck. Then change your address.

The Serial Victim is usually, not always, a victim of their own life choices and their life is a movie without an end. It's one calamity after another, one wrong decision after another. They complain about their life, a friend who talks behind their backs, mates that cheat on them, and the jobs they get fired from. They obsess about their bodies being too fat, homes that aren't as nice as some of their friends, their city which has too much crime, their country whose politics they don't like, manicurists who put on polish that peels the next day, housekeepers that steal, gardeners who peek in the windows, money that they don't have, and how the online grocery shopper got the wrong brand of toilet paper. (It's one-ply instead of two-ply, just double it up, honey.) They *even* complain about their friends that complain too much.

It doesn't matter what happens well in their life, the contentment only lasts for a day or two, and then the whining and complaining begins anew. They make you feel guilty for not doing enough for them. They can ruin your day(s) and I'm sorry to tell you, but you that life is short, then you die. No one has enough life left to spend it listening to a friend's woes constantly. You've got your own and they don't care about them.

The Martyr tells you what a good person they are, how successful they are, rich they are, popular they are, how much they give to charity, and how everyone likes them so much, so take out your BS meter. Good actions always shout louder than empty words. Eventually, you will find out that this blowhard is an egotist and not the glorified soul they claim to be. There is a saying, "Listen to people, they will tell you *who* they are." My version of this saying is "Watch peoples' actions, they will tell you *what* they really are." The Martyr will make you feel inadequate (on purpose). You don't need anyone in your life that tries to make you feel inferior. If a person is a good person, they don't need to tell you how great they are. You will know.

The Block of Ice is always very controlled, guarding their true self. An ice pick won't crack the ice, a sledgehammer won't even do the job, and they don't even make a good ice sculpture. You don't know what this person is thinking, *ever*. These ice glaciers love to give therapy hugs to show you how warm they are, but you can get frostbite from their icy hug. They are very slow and deliberate in the way they speak, move, and eat. They are nothing like they profess to be. Inside this giant ice cube, they are hiding who and what they really are, which is usually a mean, controlling, selfish, devious, and calculating imposter. *They are like a Venus Fly Trap. Beware.*

The Intellectual Snob is a self-proclaimed genius who probably couldn't pass a real IQ test without cheating, drinking Red Bull, and having a good night's sleep. Mensa Mark claims to be a genius and then does and says the dumbest things. He can't even figure out how to make money and is surprised when you tell him that he's supposed to buy low and sell high. He naively believes everything he reads is true, "because if it's written, it must be true." He reads the dictionary nightly and memorizes a big word every day so you can think is brilliant. Memorizing words is not brilliant, inventing the television or iPhone is.

Beware of obnoxious people who brag about how smart they are. Their goal is to make you feel stupid for their own glorification. Smart people don't need to tell us how smart they are and never say that they are 100% sure of anything because smart people know that there's always a small chance they are wrong. Smart people try to make *you* feel smart. We are all smart enough to recognize a genius. Just look at DumbAndDumber.com (a fake name to protect the innocent *and* the guilty) that sells phony IQ tests online.

The Narcissist loves to post lots of photos of themselves on their social media accounts. Give them a book titled "All About Me" and they're in heaven. They know enough to say, "How are you?" but don't want you to answer because they don't care. They can ramble on about themselves through a 7.2 earthquake without batting an eyelash. These self-absorbed, self-serving people don't want to see another person's view because they really don't care. They get pissed off if you question their point of view. Narcissists have a sense of entitlement and think the world revolves around them. They like to be showered with praise and go ballistic if you criticize them or even make a little suggestion. Narcissists are overly concerned about their self-image, crave constant attention, and believe they are superior and immortal. Their self-image relies upon their successes, so they bend or make up stories just to exaggerate their achievements. Narcissists lack empathy and like to prey on kind and generous people. When their self-image is threatened, they will bully and demean you in order to control you. They think they are above the law. Narcissists care about one thing, themselves. When you can no longer be of use to them, they throw you out of their lives like a used can of tuna fish.

The Ingrate is a thankless person that always asks you for favors, you grant their every wish, you even take care of their pit bull that hates you and wants to kill you while they're on vacation, you water their plants, even the fake ones, and stay at the hospital with them all day and night while their mate is ill. Then one day they ask you to pick them up from a tummy tuck and you say "Yes, of course, I will," as usual.

When the day comes their demands are so great that they would cause your mate to divorce you. The Ingrate will not understand your dilemma, nor will they bend their demands. "I'll just call another friend," they tell you snottily, forgetting that you *are* willing to pick them up. They have forgotten all the good things you have always done for them and will erase from their lives as if you are just chalk on a blackboard.

I have a client that is friends with Thankless Trudy, a woman that is always at least an hour late whenever they have plans. (When people are always late, it's an insult. They are telling you that you are not important enough for them to respect your time.) Thankless Trudy calls my client early every morning and starts babbling about her job selling bottles of water for over an hour. How much is there to say about a plastic bottle of water, you open it, you drink it, and you throw the bottle away? Like a fool, my client listens patiently every morning for an hour, 1/24th of her life. We're aging, every fraction of our life matters.

When Thankless Trudy's son is murdered, my clients rush over to take her to the morgue. *We all have a lot of things on our Bucket Lists, but I'm sure morgues are not one of them.* Next, Thankless Trudy gets a fungus in her lungs and is in the hospital about to have the third lobe removed from her lungs, my client spends her life finding a doctor that will stop her surgeon from removing it, saving her life. She never thanks my client.

My client takes her to lunch when she recovered, and she says something nasty to my client. Then my client hears through the grapevine that she was putting her down to other people and telling them that my client did nothing for her. The Ingrate is never appreciative and makes you feel that no matter what you do for them, it's not enough. As we age, we need to be appreciated for what we've done for others and to also show appreciation for what others have done for us. *You can never please in Ingrate. Move on.*

The Schemer is always trying to find a way to trick you into something that you don't want to do. You can tell a lot about your friends from their Holiday cards. Susie and Stan Schemerman were friends with one of my clients. Their Christmas cards always told their whole life's story, including how successful they were, how smart their children were, and gloated about how much more their house is now worth than last year. They were bragging, trying to make my client feel like they were better than her.

My client was tricked into going on a blind date with Susie Schemerman's cousin, Scotty Schmuck. Her's how she tells the story:

"He was nice-looking and seemed okay, *at first.*

After dinner, I went to their house to play a few games of pool. Susie insisted that we all go into the Jacuzzi. I didn't have a bathing suit with me, and I hate Jacuzzis."

"I'm tired and I'm going home now," I told her politely.

"No, I Insist!" she demanded over and over again, not letting me go.

"No, I don't want to," I screamed at her.

"You have to!" she demanded. "I'll lend you a bathing suit."

I was weak-minded and finally agreed, not thinking about the fact that Suzie is a size eighteen and I am a size two. I walked to the Jacuzzi unwillingly with a big towel around the huge bathing suit, stepped into the jacuzzi, but one of the jets was sucking the humongous bathing suit off of me and pulling it deep down into the black hole of lost bathing suits."

"I'm going home now," I announced, climbing out of the Jacuzzi, wrapping a towel around my naked body, and went upstairs to the bathroom to change back into my clothes.

Scotty Schmuck threw open the bathroom door and tried to attack me sexually. I fought him off, grabbed my clothes and ran to my car. I was tricked by the Schemerman's to have sex with their rapist cousin. It was mean and disrespectful. I felt used. No one should have friends that try to make you feel like this. As we age, we need to demand respect from everyone. If anyone treats us with disrespect, we need to get them out of our lives. *Always being treated with respect is essential to staying young and happy forever.*

The Insensitive couldn't care less about you. They make rude and mean remarks that make you feel terrible about yourself. When you are feeling down and depressed, they are talking about a football game or last week's episode of The Bachelorette (The couple that was madly in love last week broke up this week because he is now in love with a different Bachelorette.) totally unaware that you're contemplating suicide. Or, like Fart King, they throw their dirty underwear and socks on the floor for you to pick up, pretending they don't know they are demeaning and abusing you. *They know!*

They talk through you on the phone, never giving you a chance to speak. This isn't a conversation, it's a dissertation. I like to say casually, "I'm pregnant" and see if they're listening, but I've never found an Insensitive who reacts.

"With twins," I add. No reaction.

"And I'm in labor now." *Nada.*

A phone call from an insensitive is a good time to read a book or do a jigsaw puzzle. They'll never know, and if they do, who cares?

The Sociopath left their conscience and sympathy in their mother's womb along with their morals and ethics. They are usually charismatic and charming, but don't let that fool you, they are crocodiles in baby's onesies and will eat you alive.

There are many sociopaths in government,

and that's all I'm going to say about politics. The difference between a narcissist and a sociopath is that narcissists think only about themselves, but socio-paths add another dimension, they are out to hurt anyone, and I mean *anyone*, who gets in the way of their big ego and goal of achieving money, power, and control. They lie, cheat, and manipulate—even kill—in order to achieve their goals and have no remorse about hurting anyone, including you. Laws and rules are not made for sociopaths. They believe they are The Second Coming of the Big Kahuna and they're going to save the world.

The *Egocentric* feels that they are better than everyone else. They are selfish, self-centered, and have an unrealistic sense of their self-impor-tance. Egocentrics enjoy negative conversations and complain about other people a lot because it strengthens their own egos. They enjoy lots of gossip, criticism, or condemnation of others and don't take time to listen to anyone. Your point of view will never matter. Egocentrics interrupt conversations to talk about themselves because they think they're more intelligent than you and that your opinion doesn't matter. *You must always know you are important if you choose to be young and happy forever.*

The Addict can be addicted to drugs, alcohol, gambling, sex, internet porn, cheating, swindling, comfort eating, checking their social media messages constantly, hurting people or animals, anything. They like the feeling of a reward that creates a chemical release in their brain that makes them feel satisfied.

They usually have anxiety and depression and are impulsive risk-

takers. This behavior takes a toll on their relationships and health. This is usually a person who will always choose their addiction over you.

The Landmine is eruptive and unpredictable, kind of like a volcano or a nuclear bomb. You are always walking on landmines in the ground, trying not to step on one and detonate an explosion. It's way too messy to die that way. The slightest comment can set them off into a violent fiery rage over nothing. They are totally compulsive. Once I was dating this guy who was a Landmine and I said something completely innocuous, but he didn't like the tone of my voice, so he grabbed a heavy food tray and hurled it at me, just missing my head.

The Landmine can be impulsive. One time Lou and I were visiting my daughter's drug rehab along with Fart King and his third wife, his "Trophy Wife" as she liked to call herself. I once won a bowling trophy; can I call myself a trophy wife too? We were celebrating our daughter's one year sobriety chip.

I was expecting something that looked like a potato chip, but the AA reward chip looked more like a poker chip. Why would AA give out poker chips to addicts that might have gambling addiction? I had bought our daughter a huge, expensive birthday cake for everyone at the rehab. When I cut the first piece and gave it to her father (a diabetic), my daughter grabbed it from him and then dumped the whole cake in the garbage can. *I know about landmines.*

The *Nutcase* is not a case to carry your pistachios or testicles, it's a catchall term that covers all people who have a screw lose along with a lot of nuts and bolts, not to be confused with a sloppy handyman. These are the crazies who are a few face cards short of a deck. They dress weird, talk weird, move weird, and let's face it they are really "*off*". They are the hoarders, loners, loonies, eccentrics, psychos, and maniacs. These are the kind of people who will pull a gun on you if you accidentally cut them off in traffic. A nutcase in a car and a high-testosterone man in a car is like mixing drain cleaner with bleach. You get an explosion. *Warning! Don't try this!*

Lou was driving on the freeway too close behind a huge workout guy in a big pickup truck with wheels the size of a giant donut sign. The guy looked in his rear-view mirror and started pumping the brakes on and off so Lou would rear end him. Lou pulled our car around, rolled down his window and started screaming some choice words at him (bad choice words). The guy pulls out a gun and points it into our car. I was mortified and screamed bloody murder, which might be what was going to happen next. Getting away from the guy was like a high-speed police chase. We finally tricked him into getting ahead of us and quickly pulled into an off- ramp as he had just passed us. It was a narrow escape. (I changed the personalized plates on my car so he wouldn't ever find us again).

"Don't you ever do that again! I screamed hysterically.

"I won't" he promised sheepishly.

Next, we were in Santa Monica trying to find an empty parking spot, which was harder than getting into Harvard. (Unless your rich parents paid off some coach.) We finally found one parking spot after an hour and were backing up into the spot when some A-hole pulls up behind us and steals the parking spot. *Welcome to L.A.* Lou backs up, rolls down my window and starts giving this guy hell. The guy reaches down, pulls out a gun, and points it at me. I'm only a foot or two away from it with a rolled down window, which I quickly rolled up. *Who knew that a gun could shoot through a window?*

This was it, the last straw, "Get out of here fast" I screamed to Lou. I'm not going to die over a f--king parking spot!" I wasn't going to let it go unless I made him understand that if it ever happens again, he will hear from my divorce attorney. He understood clearly, except…or was it the "last straw"? *Maybe.* They had just banned straws in Los Angeles. Too many rhinoceros found with straws in their noses.

One long Memorial Day weekend we were driving from Hollywood to our home in Beverly Hills and some guy in a beat-up old car was riding our tail. This time Lou pumps the brakes on him. The guy pulls around in the next lane, rolls down the window and starts shouting nasty things at Lou, who shouts vile things back at the guy and then quickly drives away, but the Nutcase keeps following us. We couldn't get rid of him. He was right on our tail. We stopped for me to pick up my shoes from the shoemaker, Lou double parks, I went into the shoe repair shop and came back to the car. The Nutcase was still right behind him waiting for me to pick up my shoes. (He was a courteous Nutcase.) It looked like a comedy routine. We can't get rid of this lunatic. *There weren't any smartphones yet. Dumb people, yes.*

"Let's drive into the police station," I suggest to Lou as I get back into the car.

We drive into the gated courtyard in front of the Beverly Hills police station and this psycho follows us right in. I leave Lou in the car and get out, go into the police station, and tell them about this lunatic that is following us. At least twenty Beverly Hills cops ran out of the police station, guns pulled, and surrounded the guy's old beat-up junk heap. They get him out, hold him against his car, frisk him, put handcuffs on him, and take him into the police station to book him. For all we know the Nutcase is still in jail.

It is now time for all of us to get out our phone-books and *delete, delete, delete*. What will happen if we delete all these people? We will finally be happier, smile and laugh more and attract more well-centered, sane people into our lives no matter our age. *All we have to do is take action and reach out.*

CHAPTER EIGHT
Does Plastic Surgery Really Work?

I PERFORMED PLASTIC SURGERY once. I put a whole set of Tupperware on the Sani-cycle of the dishwasher. The plastic was cloudy and needed a face peel. Don't ask how that turned out. *Well, do ask.* I was scraping melted plastic out of the dishwasher for months. Dishwashing is not one of my strong points. I tried using paper plates, but it didn't work out so well when I reheated leftovers in our gas oven.

Vaginoplasty is a procedure now known more discreetly as vaginal rejuvenation, but I like to call it a vaginal remodel for women who have had too many lovers or babies in their lives. Mine's a real fixer-upper, maybe even a tear-down. I wanted to save money, so I just looked on Amazon for a vaginal tightening serum. I tried this gel called Lucky Elixir. It wasn't so lucky. Warning: don't put on too much or it might make your vagina way too tight. Try explaining it to your gynecologist or lover.

Penis enlargement is sometimes done with a penis pump that works kind of like plunging a toilet (men are good at that) or a penis implant that makes your penis look like a curved banana, which is good if your partner likes plantains. Or you might have Pyrene's disease, which you can't catch at an Italian restaurant. This disease causes your penis to be shaped like a really curved cucumber with an umbrella handle, great for tossing a salad or getting dogs toys out from under the bed.

Breast Lift surgery lifts your breasts up with a crane, removes your nipples and reattaches them to the front of your boobs so they face forward again. You now have young, perky boobs, a lot of scars, and it's easier to know where "forward" is. Be careful to choose a surgeon that is not drunk or high on drugs or God knows where your nipples will end up. BTW, seventy-year-old women aren't supposed to look like pole dancers, but older men are suckers for watermelon boobs no matter how old you are.

Rhinoplasty, contrary to popular belief, is not recommended for rhinoceros, who aren't into plastic surgery. (Rhinoceros are only interested in charging you, similar to plastic surgeons.) The Rhinoplasty, more commonly known as a nose job, should not be confused with a blow job, which is when you blow out candles on your birthday cake. The nose job is good as you age because your nose grows bigger as you age, and the size of your nose is really important when you're eighty or ninety years old. Actually, if you're not that old and the size or shape of your nose bothers you, a nose job can balance your face so that your wrinkles and thin lips don't take center stage anymore. *"Oh, you have a beautiful nose darling, but what's with all those wrinkles around your mouth?*

Liposuction, more discreetly called "body sculpting," or sucking the fat out of your huge thighs and rear-end. Nothing makes us look younger than to have a smooth tight stomach and rear-end as we age. The only problem with liposuction is that fat cells never go away, they just come back in other places, kind of like an old boyfriend who comes back with bad breath and an empty wallet. A lot of the time the fat comes back into your face, and you look like you are hiding two avocados in your mouth. Well, during a drought, avocados *are* getting scarcer. The fat cells also go into your boobs, causing your breast lift to drop, and your thighs fatten up, making you look like a well-stuffed Thanksgiving turkey.

Facelifts are an old favorite as long as you don't have your forehead lifted. Then you look like your hairline is on top of your head. If you have two forehead lifts, your eyes start popping out of your head. Three, and you look like a frog with a nice forehead.

Years ago, I decided I wanted a facelift. I didn't need one yet, but everyone I knew was getting them, so I thought it was a good idea. I consider it maintenance, like getting new tires for your old car or remodeling your kitchen.

I go in for the surgery and they wheel me into the operating room, start putting all kinds of marks on my face like they're laying out parking lot lines, give me an IV and the next thing I remember I'm lying on a bed in a recovery room with a nurse staring at my neck with horror written on her face like I was Godzilla. I heard her calling the surgeon and the anesthesiologist, who apparently had gone out for lunch together, probably to celebrate the money they made on my new face, and she was screaming into the phone, "Emergency! "Emergency! Get back here immediately! She's got a hematoma!" I was out of it and thought a hematoma might be something growing on my body, like a giant wart, or maybe just a new dance like the Macarena, but I figured something was a little wrong.

The next thing I remember is being wheeled back into the operating room, being put to sleep again, and waking up in the same recovery room with the same nurse staring with pity at my neck. I hadn't looked in the mirror yet, but the last thing I could remember is that my neck always looked like a normal neck, and I couldn't understand why she was staring at it like it was The Blob and going to jump out and attack her.

Finally, after Lou had spent all day and night waiting for me, worrying I was dead, I was picked up by a limousine and driven to a plastic surgery recovery center so I could be taken care of 24/7. This was the only time I had ever been in a limousine. It wasn't too glamourous with the bandages wrapped around my head like I was Ralph Fiennes in The

English Patient. Where were all the limousines at my two weddings or my high school prom? (Oops, I wasn't asked to my prom. Actually, I don't think I had a prom or maybe they forgot to tell me on purpose.)

I was finally alert and looked into a mirror. What I could see of my face peeking out from all the bandages was swollen and black and blue. I looked like I had gone three rounds in a boxing match with Mohammed Ali. My eyes were red with blood and there was this huge bubble sticking out of my neck like a humongous goiter. This well-fed nurse wearing a giant cross on her neck came in to bring me some food and started staring at my neck, shaking her head, murmuring *"tsk, tsk."*

"How long is it going to take for this hematoma to go away?" I asked her.

"It's in God's hands now," she replied with pity in her face.

Oh great! God can't do anything about hurricanes, earthquakes, tornados, or global warming, so I wasn't too confident he could handle a little, *well big*, hematoma. I stayed at the recovery center for three or four days and then went home. I was sentenced to go to the plastic surgeon's office every day to have my hematoma drained as if it was a can of chopped tomatoes. The more it was drained, the more it blew up with blood again. I was feeling better, so I put on a turtleneck sweater and went out to eat with good friends of ours.

We're in the car talking and laughing on our way to the restaurant and all of a sudden, my hematoma erupts and blood spurts out of my neck like Old Faithful. It was embarrassing and messy. We all laughed hysterically like we were living in an "I Love Lucy" episode.

Botox is a great idea to take all your lines away if you don't mind risking getting botulism or spending a thousand dollars a month keeping it up when nobody gives a poop whether you have a forehead like an ice-skating rink or not.

Fillers are great for smoothing out lines and plumping up your face. I actually tried having fat injected into my lips because they had gotten so thin. I walked out of the plastic surgeon's office looking like Donald Duck with a peanut allergy. I also tried fillers in the marionette lines that make me look like Edgar Bergen's dummy. The fillers kind of worked so I kept on having fillers every month or two. I gained a little weight, and the fillers were getting a little heavy. I looked in the mirror one day (not that I didn't look in the mirror every day) and I looked like a cantaloupe. So, I ran to the plastic surgeon and had him inject something that removed all the filler from my face, never to try any of this anti-aging stuff again unless it cost fifteen dollars or less from the drugstore. I don't know, maybe *au naturelle* is better. Think about it before you empty out your IRA or 401K or commit to joining a "smash and grab" gang.

So, "Does Plastic Surgery Really Work?" you ask.

"Whatever goes up must come down" is my answer.

CHAPTER NINE
Secrets of Youth and Happiness Forever

L IFE IS LIKE an elevator that goes up and down, but sometimes the power will go out and we'll get stuck in the elevator. This is the time we need to find humor in *almost* everything, depending on who you get stuck in the elevator with, of course. Life's mishaps can cause us a lot of upset, worry, and stress. This raises our blood pressure and escalates our aging process and decreases our joy of life. In order to stay young and age happily we need to laugh at these predicaments, as well as our mistakes, failures, embarrassing moments, what we look like, our sagging boobs, our limp penises, our lack of talent, our friends, our enemies, our lives, at life itself, at anything at all that can make us laugh in this upside-down world when every day is a challenge to get something done correctly. Laughing at it all reduces the stress that causes aging, unhappiness, and stress-related health problems. *How you look at life is how it looks back to you.*

Attitude is the magic key to enjoying the hand you were dealt. A positive attitude about aging will make your life happy. A negative attitude will make your life miserable. It's that simple. Make your choice.

As I showed through studies in my last book, "Choose to Be Happy: A Guide to Total Happiness", science shows that our DNA makes up for about half of our happiness and the other half of happiness is made up of nurture and attitude. Our attitude about our lives is a choice and what makes us feel happy or unhappy. As we age, we realize that not all of life can be a bowl of cherries, sometimes we get stuck with a bowl of moldy raspberries. Sh-t happens. Throw the moldy fruit in the garbage can of life and just move on.

Gratitude as we age is appreciation for our lives and what *we do have.* If we focus on what *we don't have*, we will make our lives miserable. Gratitude for even the slightest few blessings in our lives can make us feel better about aging and keep us from comparing our lives to other peoples' lives that may have ended up better than ours. We never know what goes on behind locked doors. How people present themselves on Facebook does not usually include the hurt and pain they may feel inside. Jealousy of people who have a better life than us sabotages our happiness. It makes us bitter and depressed as we age. No matter how much or how little we have, gratitude for what we do have in our lives is essential to staying young, healthy, and happy forever.

Luck is the hands we are dealt throughout our lives. It is how we handle good luck or bad luck that determines how young and happy we feel as we age. If we played our cards the best way we could with whatever knowledge we had at that time and accept that we have done the best, we can age happily. If we beat ourselves up for playing the hands we were dealt wrong, then we will most likely age unhappily and faster. Luck is just how you see your life. If you believe you are an unlucky person, you become an unlucky person. Luck is subjective. Believe you are a lucky person, and you will become a lucky person.

Hope is the magic potion that makes us look forward to tomorrow. It will help resolve the insomnia that comes with aging. It will make us want to believe that tomorrow will be great, whether it's winning the lottery (buy a ticket if you want to win, it only costs $2 to buy some hope) or hope we will get better even if we are sick, hope that our children and grand-children are well, hope that we will die painlessly, hope that we will have enough money to live out our lives, hope for a solution to global warming, to wars, to any and all suffering in the world. *Hope we will get laid again before we die*. But hope is not enough by itself. *We have to act!*

Action is the fuel that drives our engines. If we don't keep our motors running, we will become old jalopies with rusted parts that don't work anymore. Action equals achievement. We are never too old to achieve, whether it's starting a new business, writing a book, creating a beautiful garden, oil painting, joining groups and socializing, and making new friends as we age. *Action leads to purpose.*

Purpose means having goals that will make us wake up happy every day. We need to have a reason to get up every morning as we age, or we might as well stay in bed and watch the same negative news on TV over and over again. If we don't have a purpose, we need to create one, like volunteering for a charitable organization. There are lots of meaningful things we can do in life in spite of our age, health, or financial situation. If we create *attainable* goals for ourselves, we will find our purpose. It has to be realistic. If we are older, I won't mention a specific age, we're not going to become a prima ballerina or a football hero. We need to focus on the talents we were born with and finally accept the talents we will *never* have. It's about using our God-given talents, no matter what they are, to create our own definition of success and to make ourselves and other people happy at the same time. In order to fulfill your purpose, it's good to be in good health, but even if you're not, there are lots of things you can still do.

Good Health will make us enjoy life more. There is a plethora of books on staying healthy and anti-aging dos and don'ts as you age. I won't bore you with stopping smoking, eating right, exercising, and regular checkup advice. We all know that by now, even though we may still do the wrong thing. I also know that accidents and illness happen and that we may have some physical and mental handicaps, but if we use those handicaps to help others, we will find our purpose. Good health is partly genetic, and your family DNA can cause illnesses that happen even if you do everything right. Consider the last words of Steve Jobs, Apple founder, and Chairman as he was only 56 years old and lying in his sick bed dying of pancreatic cancer:

"I reached the pinnacle of success in the business world. In others' eyes my life is an epitome of success. However, aside from work, I have little joy. In the end, wealth is only a fact of life that I am accustomed to. At this moment, lying on the sick bed and recalling my whole life, I realize that all the recognition and wealth that I took so much pride in, have paled, and become meaningless in the face of impending death. You can employ someone to drive the car for you, make money for you but you cannot have someone to bear the sickness for you. Material things lost can be found. But there is one thing that can never be found when it is lost – "Life". When a person goes into the operating room, he will realize that there is one book that he has yet to finish reading – "Book of Healthy Life." Whichever stage in life we are at right now, with time, we will face the day when the curtain comes down. Treasure Love for your family, love for your spouse, love for your friends...Treat yourself well. Cherish others. As we grow older, and hence wiser, we slowly realize that—wearing a $300 or $30 watch - they both tell the same time...Whether we carry a $300 or $30 wallet/handbag - the amount of money inside is the same; Whether we drive a $150,000 car or a $30,000 car, the road and distance is the same, and we get to the same destination. Whether we drink a bottle of $300 or $10 wine - the hangover is the same; Whether the house we live in is 300 or 3000 sq. ft. - loneliness is the same. You will realize your true inner happiness does not come from the material things of this world. Whether you fly first or economy class, if the plane goes down - you go down with it... Therefore, I hope you realize, when you have mates, buddies and old friends, brothers and sisters, who you chat with, laugh with, talk with, have sing songs with, talk about north-south-east-west or heaven and earth, ... That is true happiness!!"

— Steve Jobs

Resilience is what makes us keep going no matter what happens. When life gives you rotten fruit, make compost. We need resilience to get us through all the bad things that may happen to us as we age. Resilience is born out of hope and purpose. Resilience is the rubber band of our life that holds us

91

together. The trick is to keep the rubber band from breaking with humor and laughter.

Love is a gift we need to give before we can receive it. It is an emotion that gets stronger with age, not something we fall into. That's just infatuation. As we grow older, our sense of self, empathy, sympathy, morality, ethics, and sensitivity develops and we become stronger, better, kinder, and more loving people. Our intuition usually gets stronger too and we are able to detect red flags easier. We get wiser with age.

There are always those who never experience this growth. Most everything in our world has a Ying and a Yang. There is up and down, right, and left, chocolate and vanilla, cold and hot, far and near, hard and soft (well, you get my point). It is logical then that if there is a God there must be a Satan. God is about creating love, beauty, and joy. Satan is about destroying love, beauty, and joy. It's the perfect cast of characters for our Creator's very long and complicated game of chess.

Some people never find true love unfortunately. It is usually because they haven't learned to love themselves. You can't love another person if you don't love yourself. In the same way, you can't find happiness if you don't know what makes you happy. No one can love themselves if they don't show the world who they really are. If you can't be honest with another person, how can they love you for what you are if you are not who you say you are? People who find mates as they age don't false advertise. No photoshopping! No made-up stories! No lies! No more false fronts! (Okay, breast implants, facelifts, and hair transplants excluded.) If you are true to yourself and who you are and present your genuine self, you can find a mate at any age. Finally, being yourself as you age is very liberating. *Love and self-honesty will brighten up your life and make you feel younger, happier, and healthier no matter what your age.*

Acceptance of ourselves and our lives is the only way we can live a long, joyful life. When we accept our own flaws, we can better accept the flaws of others. Life rarely turns out exactly the way we want it to turn out for most of us. How our lives turn out is contingent on all our successes, mistakes, and sometimes just pure good or bad luck. In order to enjoy the rest of our lives, we need to accept the past and what has happened or not happened to us. We need to accept the inevitable, which includes death. So, go ahead and laugh yourself to death. What we don't accept turns into fear. Acceptance is one of the qualities that can make our lives a lot easier and more peaceful as we age. *Embrace change if you want to feel younger, happier, and healthier.*

My daughter showed me this Alcoholics Anonymous quote years ago, "Grant me the serenity to accept the things I cannot change, the courage to change the things I can, and the wisdom to know the difference." — Alcoholics Anonymous p. 40-41 "The greatest enemies of us alcoholics are resentment, jealousy, envy, frustration, and fear." (Yes, she was a drug addict, but I'm proud to say she's turned her life around.)

My client, David Downer, was a good-looking, healthy man who enjoyed the good life of mingling with Hollywood celebrities and dating beautiful women, Playmates of the Month were his specialty. Now that he is in his eighties, he is constantly complaining about all the normal physical problems that most people experience as they age. He is bitter and resents not being able to still have the life he used to enjoy instead of trying to enjoy the life he has left now. David is stuck in the days gone by and tells the same old stories of his past life over and over again. He is lonely and has a bad time performing the normal tasks people do if they live alone. Everything is all too much for him. I try to get him to accept aging.

"Everyone has these problems as they age and they learn to accept them, even laugh at them, if they choose to enjoy what is left of their lives," I say to him kindly.

"I'm not everybody, I will not accept aging!" he answers stubbornly, as if he has a choice, and then goes back to telling me over and over again about how his wonderful his life used to be.

I am frustrated. How life used to be is *never* what it still is. Feeling younger and happier requires accepting that we are all aging together and learning to enjoy and laugh at it. You can't age backwards, so the only way to stop aging is to die. *That's really not the best solution.* Giving up is like watching a great whodunit movie and falling asleep before you find out whodunit. I certainly don't want him or anyone else who feels like this to die, and he doesn't want to die either, so there is only one answer to living happily as we age, and that is to accept reality and deal with the ailments and frustrations that most all of us experience as we get older.

Another client, Stubborn Sally, is a single woman approaching sixty years old who also can't accept aging. She thinks she looks younger than she is and wants a mate that is much younger than her, "not a decrepit old man" in her words.

"I'd rather be alone than settle for a man I don't love," she declares.

"Most younger men want a younger woman to start a family," I tell her.

"I'm not going to settle!" she exclaims emphatically. "I'm unhappy because I don't like the way my life turned out and I'm lonely."

I wanted to pull out my hair, but I realized I hardly had any left. It's a catch-22. She has made a huge effort to improve herself and her life and that's great, but unless she accepts that she is aging and realizes that life doesn't always give you the life you had wanted and accepts the life she does have, she will never be able to enjoy her life. As she keeps on aging, finding a mate and happiness will just get more difficult. Of course, you *can* find a mate at any age. Another client of mine has a mother who is over one-hundred years old and lives in an assisted living facility with a boyfriend she met there. (I don't know whether they still have sex or not. I probably shouldn't ask.)

Forgiveness makes us free of anger. If we feel shame or guilt about ourselves, we need to forgive ourselves finally, let go, and move on. If someone has hurt us, let's forgive them, let go and move on. Forgiving someone that has mistreated us doesn't change the person that hurt us, but it makes our lives happier as we age. Releasing our bodies and souls from the burden of inner anger emancipates us so we can enjoy the life we still have left. Let's learn to laugh about the people we were naïve enough to let into our lives, or the family and relatives that we are obliged to put up with. Let's find humor in everything and everybody in our lives. It feels so much better than crying and self-pity. Savor the good memories and let go of the bad ones. Let's live life in the now. We can't change the past and we can't predict the future, so all we have is today. *Forgiveness will set us free.*

When I was twenty-one, I was in the hospital and alone with my father while he was dying of cancer of the larynx that had spread. I knew it was the end. I held his hand as he died, kissed his forehead, and said "I love you." I drove home crying and forgave him for all the things he had done to me, or maybe perceived he had done to me. Forgiveness is always the right thing to do.

Truth is the authenticity that gives us peace and earns us the respect of others. If we lie about ourselves and our achievements, we are liars. If we tell stories that aren't true, we are liars. If we lie about something bad we did, or some mistake we made, we are liars. If our lies are found out, we become fools and may spend the rest of our lives in a penitentiary laundry ironing orange jumpsuits.

If we don't discover our true selves as we age, we may die never knowing who or what we really were and what good we were capable of doing for society. Our true self is the us that feels comfortable in our own skin, that has nothing to prove, no one to impress, and makes us free to enjoy the life that makes *us* happy, not the life that society says will make us happy. Truth is the pesto in the pesto sauce. *Truth is the freedom to be the real you.*

Honesty Wis the truth serum that feeds our self-love, self-respect, and self-worth as well as respect from others as we age. It is the main ingredient of good relationships with others and ourselves. Without honesty, we are imposters, a form of identity theft. It's simple, just be yourself. You will be surprised how many people will be drawn to you when you strip away your onion peel and reveal the bare onion bulb of your true self to them. *Life opens up for you no matter what age you are if you are honest and truthful.*

Integrity gives us self-esteem. If we age with integrity, we will always do the right thing even if no one else notices. We can give to charity without bragging about it, and always try to make others feel good about themselves. We will not do anything that will hurt any human or animal no matter what they have done to us. *Vengeance is toxic to our souls and makes it impossible to age younger, happier, and healthier.*

Kindness is like a boomerang. Throw it out and it comes right back to us to make us feel special and worthy. If we open doors for people older than us or handicapped, watch them smile and say, "Thank you". Thank strangers who served in the military for their service and risked their lives for us and watch them smile with pride. Be kind to service workers and drivers that work so hard to make our lives easier, and we will make their day worthwhile. Kindness is a free unlimited commodity that never takes anything away from us but always adds joy to our lives and to other peoples' lives. Just smile at everyone and see how it works like magic. *No matter how old we are, kindness will transform our lives and keep us young and happy.*

Intuition is the best tool we have to guide us through a happier, healthier, and safer life as we age. The good news about aging is that our intuition gets stronger and stronger. Small red flags become great big red waving flags. These are omens from your Life Concierge.

When Lou and I were skiing at Alta Utah. I went up some wood stairs with a wood railing to go to the bathroom. On the way down I put my hand on the railing and got a big wood splinter in my hand. We went to the First Aid room, but they didn't have any tweezers. After they finally found a needle and got the splinter out, I said to Lou, "What else could happen?" I was about to find out. What I've learned aging is to *never ask* "What else could happen?" because it always does if we don't pay attention to the omens.

Later that day we were at the top of a gentle slope, skiing down, enjoying the run. Coming at me fast from a side run and out of control, was this very tall, muscular young guy, probably stoned. He had locked his eyes on my bright purple ski jumpsuit. (I know I shouldn't have bought that purple ski suit. I spent too much on it and now I'm being punished.) This guy was skiing right at me like an out-of-control Kamikaze pilot. No matter how fast and far I skied to get out of his way, he was speeding right into me.

It felt like a cement truck hit me. I was in shock. I was lying on the ground screaming in pain. Part of my right leg was sticking out of my thick jumpsuit pants. There was blood everywhere. I didn't realize it was my blood.

The Ski Patrol girl lifted me into one of those rescue baskets to take injured skiers down the mountain. I had seen injured skiers being brought down the hill in those rescue baskets and I had always wanted to know what it was like to be inside one. It was bumpy and painful. The Ski Patrol girl kept looking back as she skied down the hill and asking me, "How are you doing?"

"Great." I replied. *How the f--k do you think I'm doing?*

Some cute guys in EMT uniforms loaded me on a gurney and stuck me inside an ambulance. I had never been inside an ambulance, so I saw it as a learning experience. They took me to some hut, pulled my ski boots off over my broken forty-five-degree angle leg, and shoved a big fat tetanus shot needle into my arm. I screamed. Screaming is okay. What's the use of being in pain if no one knows about it?

I was lifted into another ambulance and transported to some hospital in Sandi, Utah, wherever that is. Nurse Misery cut off my designer purple ski jumpsuit that I loved and insisted I pee into a bedpan. I couldn't no matter how hard I tried. I was still in shock. She got pissed at me (pun intended) and stormed out of the room. Just what I needed, a nurse with "issues."

Several surgeons walked in. They were very nice, explained that I had an open spiral compound fracture of my tibia as well as a fracture of my fibula and that I would be in the operating room for about eight hours at least and not to worry, they would take good care of me. *Easy for them to say.* They stuck an IV in my arm and wheeled me into the operating room.

I woke up upstairs in a hospital room with metal hardware outside my leg holding it together. My leg looked like one of those big outdoor TV antennas. *Was I going to have to wear this hardware all my life? How would I wear my jeans or skirts? Would I get free TV reception from my leg?*

The next day I had another surgery to put my leg back together and insert a titanium rod through it. *Oh great. Now I would set off the metal detectors at the airport and they would think I was going to blow up the plane.* After two weeks, I got to go home. The good news is they gave me a bulkhead seat because I couldn't bend my leg. *Every cloud has a silver lining.*

Once home, a friend insisted I needed to "juice" to heal. She went to Whole Foods (like other markets sold food that wasn't whole) and bought me the most expensive juicer and every kind of vegetable and fruit known to mankind, with my credit card. She started making juice for two hours, tossing all the pulp and seeds and skin and whatever fruit and vegetables were made of on the kitchen counter. How did she expect me to stand in the kitchen for two hours to make juice for myself when I needed to walk with two crutches and had sore red armpits already? I got my huge credit card bill, a juicer I never used, and had enough fruits and vegetables to cure scurvy forever.

As I healed somewhat, I was able to drive and take myself to physical therapy with crutches. The physical therapist's assistant, who didn't bother to read my case notes, insisted I had to do this exercise with rubber bands on my ankle. This broke the two screws in my ankle that held the rod inside my tibia. The next thing I know is I'm at a hospital again, having operation number three in order to remove the broken screws from my ankle. I wasn't quite under the anesthesia yet and I saw two surgeons walk in with saws big enough to amputate my leg. I thought they were going to dismember me and stuff my body parts in a barrel and throw me in the Pacific Ocean.

Then my broken fibula wasn't healing, and my new orthopedist told me they would have to saw my fibula apart so that it would heal. I felt like a victim in the Texas Chainsaw Massacre movie.

I hobbled with crutches to the juice store for wheat grass juice every day and finally it healed. Now I am left with a metal rod in my right leg with two screws in my knee holding it in and am miserable in cold weather and set off the machines at the airport. If the price of metals keeps on going up, I'm going to be worth a fortune. If only I had listened to my intuition about the tweezers. I think this *almost* proves my point about listening to omens.

Red Flags and Omens. Charley, our Airedale, passed away from kidney disease. We wanted a mini-Airedale, so we decided to buy a seven-month-old Lakeland Terrier from a breeder we found on the Internet. It was weird that she had three unsold seven-month-old puppies (*Red Flag!)* but what the heck. We drove about 130 miles to buy a new puppy.

An elderly woman and her grown daughter greeted us kind of oddly, like they had a dead body stuffed in the closet. We sat in the living room and saw a big towel covering something on the carpet. *Aha! Covering up blood stains. Another Red Flag!* I have watched too many episodes of Dateline.

The mother brings out the two "bitches", a name given to female dogs by a misogynist. They were very cute, but way too high-strung, so the mother puts the bitches away. I walk out to the backyard for a minute, see the mother holding the bitch tightly in her lap with one hand over its eyes. Apparently, the stud and the bitch were having relationship problems and she was keeping them apart. *Aha, yet another Red Flag!* We ignored this one too unfortunately.

The daughter brings out the "stud," the name for a male dog, thought up by a dancer at Chippendales. He was the cutest puppy. His tail was wagging fast, and he jumped in my lap, rolled over, and asks for a belly rub, kind of like a man on a first date after he bought you an expensive dinner. He had the cutest ass too. We named him Bernie. We were about to find out that Bernie was doing a con job on us, like some psychopath we met on the Internet.

Bernie endeared himself to us over the first few months. We put a towel under his food bowl in the kitchen, so he started covering up his food with the towel. *How cute, he's saving it for later. Maybe we should have given him some Tupperware to keep it in.* Then we gave him a big bone to gnaw on. *Bad idea.* He took that bone everywhere and if we got near him, he started to growl and grit his teeth and looked like he was going to kill us if we got close to him. We became prisoners in our own home.

One morning he was lying on our bed with his eyes wide open, looking so sweet and innocent, so I leaned down to kiss him sweetly. *Big Mistake!* (I'm human. I make mistakes.) Suddenly he jumps up, grabs me by my lower lip, bites down as hard as he can, and I'm walking around screaming with a dog hanging onto my lips, blood pouring from my mouth. He looked like one of those performers who hangs onto a long rope with her teeth and twirls fast like an ice skater. Bernie turned out to be the Ted Bundy of the canine world.

I spent the rest of the day at UCLA Emergency Room with an IV of morphine as they injected me with Novocain and two plastic surgeons sewed up my lips for three hours. Now I look like a have a forever-herpes looking sore on my lips. *Oops! I did it again. Another learning experience. Pay attention to the red flags!*

CHAPTER TEN
Myths about Aging

MYTH NUMBER ONE: *If you are rich, you will age happily.* Get real! Money can make you happy and lack of money can make you unhappy, but money alone cannot make you happy. I know plenty of unhappy rich people. As I've aged, I have learned firsthand that the happiest people are those who are rich in friends and family, not the people who think expensive possessions and pretentious friends will make them happy.

We don't need a lot of money to cultivate new friends that are on Team Good. There are places of worship, senior citizen groups, free lectures at the library, gardening clubs, and lots of clubs you can join. *Pass on the Klu Klux Klan.* You don't need a lot of money to write a book, volunteer for a charitable cause, or work on a political campaign. You will be rich if you give back to society and help make it a better world in any small (or big) way. What I have learned while sitting in so many doctors' waiting rooms is that too many people, even younger people, have given up. They haven't taken care of their bodies, and many are too obese to walk without a cane, a walker, or even one of those motorized carts. (I almost got run over by one in the market.) They look miserable and don't care how they look, wear old wrinkled, mismatched clothing and worn-out shoes. Their sad faces show their pain and hopelessness. Please don't give up! *You are never too old to find happiness, laugh again, and regain your youthfulness.*

Myth Number Two: Success will make you happy. Success has a different meaning for each person. Some people think of success as making a lot of money even if they have screwed other people in the process. Feeling all-powerful and controlling everyone will not make you happy. Feeling physically attractive will not make you happy forever. In time, physical beauty declines no matter how much plastic surgery. A kind soul *will* make you happy and beautiful forever no matter how old you are. Kind people get more attractive as they age. Mean people get uglier as they age.

A mean soul can turn into a kind soul if it's not a mental disorder or disease. If you are thinking or starting to do or say something mean, stop yourself before you do or say it. Rewrite it in your head. Happy, kind, and intelligent people always think before they say or do something that will hurt another person or an animal. Think before you speak!

To us less self-absorbed mortals (well, to be honest, I'm still a little vain) success is just a good feeling about what we do, whether it's a menial job, volunteering to help others, hiking, enjoying the beauty of the earth, gardening, playing cards, or just having a handful of good friends to laugh and hang out with. A wonderful family is a plus, but if we don't have our own family, making our friends into our families helps. It doesn't matter what makes us happy if we're happy, unless of course we are not hurting animals and killing people or conning trusting people out of their money. Consider the following poem by Ralph Waldo Emerson.

> *To laugh often and much To win*
> *the respect of intelligent people*
> *and the affection of children; To*
> *earn the appreciation of honest*
> *Critics and endure the betrayal of false*
> *Friends; To appreciate beauty, to find*
> *the best in others; To leave the world a*
> *bit better, whether by a healthy child,*
> *a garden patch or a redeemed social*
> *condition; To know even one life has*
> *breathed easier because you*
> *have lived.*
> *This is to have succeeded.*
> *. . . Ralph Waldo Emerson*

Myth Number Three: Age is only a number. Ridiculous, unless it's the number of doctors you've seen and hospitals you've been in. In this case, *The less, the better.* I used to have a young trainer at my health club, and he tried to push me to my physical limit and say to me, "You're only as old as you think you are." He was young and it was easy for him to say. I get it. But f--k you Troy, old *is* old. We can't do as much as we used to be able to do, but that's okay. Once we accept our limitations and learn to do just as much as we can, we can finally enjoy our lives without always thinking we should do more. *Accept your limitations.*

Myth Number Four: You'll enjoy your Golden Years. You may not have a retirement unless you've been smart and lucky enough to stash enough money to keep up your standard of living. Many of us have lost a lot of money in the stock market in recent years or invested it in some con artists get-rich scheme. (Shouldn't they be called *con magicians* because they make your money disappear?) Or you've spent all your money on your children, grandchildren, or medical expenses, so now you still have to make enough money to live out your life. Thanks to medical science, life expectancy has increased by twenty years, so now you have to figure out how to make enough money for that extra twenty years.

Figure twenty years extra age expectancy at 8.7% inflation and you'll see what I mean. If you've bought toilet paper lately (and I hope you have since there are no old phone books or newspapers to use anymore) you'll know that the price of toilet paper is astronomically high. Toilet paper manufacturers are now selling used toilet paper. They call it "recycled". Who recycles toilet paper? I think I'm going to recycle ours and try to sell it on eBay. It'll save on our water bill because we won't have to flush. And now there's bamboo toilet paper so you can grow bamboo shoots out of your rear-end, like a Chia Pet.

Worrying about making enough money keeps you active and your brain alert as you age. Living in a retirement home playing bingo gets old and so will you. If you think young and live as if you're young, you will feel young. Stop worrying and make life more complicated than it has become. Use your brain power to think young and make money doing something you enjoy.

Myth Number Five: People don't have sex when they're old. Don't be naïve. People still have sex well into their seventies and beyond. I know a woman who had three men die on her while having sex. They called her Killer. *True.* At least they died doing what they loved to do.

People who have mates live longer, and if they are having sex, they live even longer. According to *Psychology Today*, English researchers surveyed the sexual frequency of 918 seniors who still had sex. Men who had sex twice a week increased their life span by ten years. *Of course, the women died ten years younger.*

According to another study in *Psychology Today*, a full third of seniors reported that they were having sex more often than the average for the younger generation. "In other words, a significant portion of older adults had a sex life that would make most young adults envious!" *See, ninety is the new twenty!* Senior sex can also burn calories (if you move), reduces the risk of heart disease, regulates hormone levels, cures headaches and reduce pain, reduces stress, and lowers blood pressure, reduces the risk of prostate cancer (only if you're a male), reduces the risk of breast cancer (both sexes), boosts self-esteem and improves mood, improves the sense of smell (not necessarily a good thing if you your mate passes a lot of gas), and increases bladder control.

If you don't have a mate, I've thought about inventing an artificial penis that whispers sweet nothings in your ear, so I made a prototype. The problem was that I couldn't fit the artificial penis is my ear. Then I thought I'd manufacture micro-mini earplugs that whisper sweet nothings in your ears, and I made another prototype, but my hearing was getting so bad couldn't hear the sweet nothings. Now I just talk to myself.

Myth Number Six: You can trust most anyone. Nope! As we grow older and age, we need to sharpen our *trust* antennas. This brings me back to my theory of good and evil. Half of the people in this world are shades of good (Team Good) and can be trusted and the other half of people are shades of bad (Team Bad) and can't be trusted. This gives you a 50/50 chance of getting hurt. People on Team Evil will do anything to anyone in order to profit from it in some way. They don't care who they hurt. Team Good and Team Evil don't wear T-shirts to identify themselves. There is no vaccination yet to protect us from bad people. Learning to read people and their motives is one of the most important ways we can survive the jungle without getting too badly hurt. It takes time and develops over the years as we age. We must learn from our mistakes in order to survive and age happily.

Internet fraud is growing. Accessing your smart-phone, text messages, emails, and social media accounts are the major ways that predators get into your life and fool you into making a big mistake with your money, or even your life. Criminals don't need to rob banks anymore. Learn the tricks that scammers use to steal your money by tricking you. One popular way scammers use is to email or text you in order to get you to click on links that will take you to their phony websites. Then they tell you to put in your personal information. This allows them access to your private financial accounts. *Do not click on anything in an email or text!* Only use official websites with a high security icon and the letters https: in front of their Internet addresses from companies you know and trust.

Then there are the robocalls that try to talk you into taking out a student loan or a warranty on your car. Be aware of new people who message you with "Hi, Beautiful" especially if you're a man that's not gay. A good idea is to sign up for a service that blocks most of these scammers but be sure the service you choose is not a scam too. The Internet has become a cyber jungle.

As we age most of us learn to *never* trust blindly and we become more *Intuitive*. I've learned the hard way. Look at facial expressions, body movements, words matching emotions, how a person treats other people, how they treat animals. Learn to trust your *Intuition* when you notice something that's off-putting or weird. Remember, our *Intuition* is almost always right. If it doesn't *feel* right, it's not right. I've learned the hard way.

Myth Number Seven: Old people lose their memories. You don't have to get old and senile! You don't even have to lose your memory, and even if you forget a few things, there are always post-Its to remind you of everything you need to do and clutter up your house. (I once put so many post-Its on my refrigerator door that I couldn't find the door, so I just went out to eat for a year.)

Brain boosters can't really be bought at a vitamin store. There is even one popular brand of brain enhancer pills that contain jellyfish. (Great for multi-tasking.) Unfortunately, you'll get stung by the price and maybe even grow tentacles. The only way to stay young and enhance your memory is to keep your brain and body active. Your brain cells will deteriorate faster as you age if you don't exercise your brain every day, whether it's playing the piano or cards or doing crossword puzzles along with taking walks and lifting light weights. Dancing, yoga, and Pilates are great for anti-aging. So is sex and it doesn't require special clothes.

Myth Number Seven: Old people get grumpy. Grumpy isn't a prerequisite for getting old, although there are a lot of cantankerous older people out there. Sex works! So does getting out of the house and doing anything (well, not exactly anything, masturbating in a park full of children isn't such a good idea.)

Myth Number Eight: Old people can't think for themselves. BS. Old people *aren't* ready for the glue factory. Lithium-ion pioneer John Goodenough helped spark the wireless revolution as the oldest person to receive a Nobel prize at ninety-seven. Older people may not think as fast as young people because their brains are so full of information.

As we get older, we can get a little confused because life is getting more and more complicated every day. There are too many choices and things to do and too little energy to do them. We get stressed much easier than younger people because changes in our world and our lives are happening too quickly for us to adjust to them. Life is getting faster as we're getting slower. Don't stress yourself out. Go at your own pace and you'll feel younger, happier, and healthier.

Myth Number Nine: Old people have a lot of money stashed away. Don't bet on it if you're hanging around for a big inheritance! Inflation has driven up the costs of elder care. The average cost of assisted living in the United States is over $4,000 per month and can be over $7,000 and the average cost of nursing homes is about $8000 a month. Some can be as much as $13,000 a month.

Using the statistic that people are living twenty years longer than previous generations, the cost of living ten of those years in an assisted living facility is about $500,000 and living ten of those years in a nursing facility is $1,000,000 for a total of $1,500,000 to live those extra twenty years. This is certainly a good reason to keep yourself healthy and happy and exercise your brain and body every day and buy the best long-term care insurance you can buy if you can afford it.

CHAPTER ELEVEN
How Not to Sabotage Your Life

HATE IS A dirty word! Hating everyone only makes everyone hate you, and even makes you hate yourself. What you put out in the Universe is what you get back. If you throw poop against a wall, some of it will bounce back and hit you in the face. Hating others is a cancer on your soul. Feeling hate makes *you* feel bad. The person you hate is probably toxic and doesn't know or doesn't give a monkeys rear-end you hate them. Hate also hurts your health and ability to age happily and have a fun-filled life.

As you get older, it's time to let go of all your old grudges, animosities, hatreds, grievances, feelings of revenge, and any other negative feelings about other people in your life and replace them with under-standing, forgiveness, and love. Now is a good time to contact all these people and make peace. It may work out and you will reconnect, or they may not be receptive, but you have made the effort that will free your body and soul of toxic feelings, making room for happiness and laughter. Remember, happiness and laughter are magnets and draw other happy people into your life, so letting go of hate attracts a lot of new and more positive friends.

People who hate themselves project their dislike of themselves onto others or inanimate objects. They have eliminated any joy in their lives and refuse to take up any hobbies or interests. These are people that refuse to try anything new, make new friends, or to go to new places. They have removed any chance of joy and happiness in their lives and are doomed to a lonely, unhappy life. My advice to these people is to lighten up your heart and let go of all the people and things and places you hate, get the toxic people out of your life, and get out there and find things you love to do, people you love to be with, and make an effort to turn your life around before it's too late and you die alone with regret in your heart.

Denial. Some people are stuck in the quicksand of the past. They don't understand that being young and happy as you age doesn't mean dressing like a teenager, smoking pot, and going to rave parties. It means aging gracefully and thinking young and joyful. You can feel young and adventurous and laugh and have fun no matter how old you are.

The first clue that a person is in aging denial is how they dress. Did you ever see an older woman who is glued to how she looked fifty years ago when she was the prom queen? Her dyed blonde hair is teased up in a "bubble" and she's wearing a push-up bra, exposing a saggy crêpe cleavage under her polyester print blouse that she thinks is hiding her expanding waist and bloated stomach. Her cellulite is covered up by a pair of 100% Spandex yoga pants that pulls in her obvious bulges. She's wearing three-inch heels because she's shrinking but can barely walk. She keeps on falling, but she doesn't want anyone to know she's losing her balance. Her face is painted with a thick foundation and a bright purple shadow is smeared on her eyelids. She bats her false eyelashes at you as if two hummingbirds just landed on her lids. Her main accessory is a fake Chanel bag she bought on sale on eBay.

Dressing appropriate for our age doesn't mean we aren't youthful anymore; it means we are in sync with our age and don't want to look silly. Dressing like we're still in high school and trying to look "cool" just draws attention to the fact that we've gotten older.

Men who are stuck in their glory years as a college football star like to wear baseball caps with sayings like "Marines" to cover their bald heads, a floral print shirt that covers their IBS-C inflated belly, and khaki cargo shorts exposing their white hairless legs. When they get dressed up, they wear slacks pulled up to their armpits or a polyester leisure suit from the seventies.

We are well into the twenty-first century and as we get older, it's silly to try to look like we looked in high school or college. We start to forget things, like why we just walked into a room, what doctors we're supposed to see on what day, or that we accidentally let our teapot boil all day and our kitchen has burnt down. *So, we'll eat out.* We're shrinking too. It's kind of obvious when you pull on a pair of pants and the hem is dragging on the floor or a blouse or suit jacket that could fit a puppy in each shoulder where your muscles used to be. (Warning, do not try this, the puppy might poop or smother.)

Do you remember how older people looked to us when we were young? Did we not treat them with the kindness and respect they deserved? Well, guess what, we're those older people or soon to be older people now. Guess what, there's Karma.

Growing older doesn't mean you have to be stuck in times long gone when you were younger and in your prime. Don't be in denial. Let go of the past, live for today and your future because it's all you have left no matter how old you are. You can be full of life at any age. Inflexibility of your body is normal as you age, but inflexibility of your mind is not. When you imprison yourself into a self-locking cage and refuse to learn and accept new concepts, you lock yourself out of a chance to be happy and enjoy the rest of your life. Break open that cage and let yourself out to enjoy new and exciting places, people, and experiences. It's like polishing up old, tarnished silver until it shines brilliantly. You're the star of your own life, you can either fade away or shine brightly forever.

Resentment. Like a lot of my clients, life hasn't

always been good to me. I know a lot of you may come from abusive homes, or survived some horrible illness, or have some type of disability, or are from poverty. A lot of you have lived through a lot of tougher experiences than I have, but hopefully you've all had some good experiences. Whatever hand you've been dealt, however old you are, it's time to turn that hand into a winning hand. The past is gone, the future is unknown, so today is all we have to live our lives with joy and gratitude. Let go of the past, deal with the problems that are sure to arise almost every day and enjoy what you can as you age. Resentment of the hand you were dealt and blaming something that happened to you in the past is a recipe for unhappiness, health problems, and premature aging. Don't dwell on bad memories. Work hard on good new memories.

Negativity is another magnet. Pessimistic thoughts attract unfavorable experiences. After my divorce I did what all divorcees did, I got my real estate license. I would take prospective buyers on tours of houses and point to rooms. "This is the living room, this is the dining room, this is the den, this is the bathroom, this is the bedroom, it's a great price," I would tell them. At the real estate office, I tried making some cold calls to get new listings. My sales pitch was "You wouldn't like to sell your house, would you?" Salesperson of the month I would never be. I think I was fired.

Failure. There is no such thing as failure as long as when something doesn't work out, we pick ourselves up, wipe off the tears, brush off the dust, and try something else no matter how old we are. We only fail if we stop trying, so don't stop trying and you'll never be a failure.

Of course, money isn't all that important until you no longer have any. The "less is more" theory doesn't apply when it comes to money. Money becomes essential to your existence. *It wouldn't happen to me, I always thought, but it did. It can happen to anyone in this upside-down unpredictable world.* When your financial statement said you were worth three million dollars not too long ago and you've lost everything and your bank account is down to your last $400, you know you did something wrong or have very bad luck. I know because that's exactly what happened to us. Laughing and making jokes about our financial position gave me the hope and strength to pull us out of it. I started a successful online business, and all was going great until…

The dollar was going up fast after the 2016 presidential election and our income was going down even faster because of the strong dollar. I lost all of my international income, which was 75% of my sales. I had a stroke that I didn't know was a stroke. I couldn't work as hard as I had been working. It was too expensive to live in Los Angeles anymore, so we were forced to move to Las Vegas where the rent was one-third of what it was in Los Angeles. I still had the rest of my sales and Lou made a little money brokering preowned auto parts, so we would be able to survive, although even bugs or insects can't even survive in Las Vegas because it's so hot.

We fell in love with a large two-story house on a beautiful tree-lined gated community and signed the lease, went back to L.A., gave notice, and packed up everything and moved to Las Vegas. It seemed like our only logical option, but life had a different plan for us. Failure was not an option, but maybe it could be. None of us know what our future will bring, good or bad. *I'm an optimist, but I'm also a realist.*

The day before our move I felt fine. The movers were there all day and some of our neighbors (the ones who didn't hate us or weren't terrorists) came by and everything was great. Once the movers were done, we went to the Horror Hotel, (name changed to protect the guilty) to stay the night before we left for our new life in Las Vegas. I had made the room reservations on some online travel website, so I thought we were all set. *Think again.* The nasty clerk, Miss Doodyface, at the front desk of Horror Hotel asked me accusingly, "Did you make the reservations on Fiasco.com?" (Name changed to protect the guilty too.)

"Yes," I replied, feeling condemned for some crime I didn't commit. She looked at me as if I was a criminal on the run. "You didn't make the reservations on the Horror Hotel website?"

"Nope," I confessed to the awful crime she was suggesting I had perpetrated.

Her face tightened up and she sucked in her breath, hell bent on punishing me for not making the reservations directly on the Horror Hotel website. *How was I to know it was a sin? I was willing to go to confession.*

"I'm sorry" I replied, scared that Fiasco.com was some evil website on the deep dark web I had accidentally stumbled upon.

She looked at me with disgust. "You can only have a 'standard king'," she said snidely, as if I was smuggling cocaine into Mexico.

"What is a 'standard" king," I inquired.

"It's smaller than a regular king," she sneered.

"How small?" I asked nicely.

"Adequate," she replied snottily.

"How small could it be?" I asked carefully as if I was asking a man about the size of his penis.

"Tolerable" she said, not really caring whether I lived or died. At that point I didn't care either.

"Okay," I said, exhausted from moving all day.

Lou and I went out to our SUV, *short for shitty underpowered vehicle*, to get our suitcases. Lou had put a huge bottle of prune juice in his suitcase, enough to cure the constipation of the entire Chinese army, and it had spilled out in our suitcases and the trunk of our car. Now we were the Prune People.

We put the hotel key in the lock, opened the door into a closet with a bed in it. The dresser was on one wall with about eight inches of space for us to squeeze by and get into the bed. We collapsed on a saggy bed and fell asleep. When I got up in the morning, we had to meet our landlord and give him back his keys, so

I rushed to get showered in this tiny bathroom meant for a miniature human or a large chihuahua.

I felt a little woozy and weird and had to lay down a little bit, but we were running late. I put on the same clothes I had been wearing, everything else was soaked in prune juice. Lou was rushing me, so I tried to slide between the dresser and the bottom of the bed, but my body kept pulling me down as if the devil was pulling me down into hell. *Maybe he was? Or maybe the devil is she? Or trans?* I never thought I was going to go to hell, but it must be that Little Lulu comic book I stole when I was five years old.

Lou told me to hurry up. *Sure Lou. I'm being pulled down into to the depths of hell and you want me to hurry up. Who hurries up on their way to hell?* The force pulling my right arm down got stronger and stronger and I fell, getting crushed eight inches between the bed and the dresser. We had to return the landlord's keys. *Please God, give me the strength.* I had to find my resilience, which I think was in the trunk of our car soaked in prune juice.

Next, we had to pick up Lulu at Deborah's, our pet sitter. She just hugged me and started to cry when she saw me. I had no idea why. I felt something really weird had happened to me, but I didn't know that I was lisping terribly and completely out of it and uncoordinated. *I was always clumsy anyway.* I found out a few months later what had happened to me.

We got to the hotel in Las Vegas, I felt a little weird, but I was functioning. The next morning, the movers were waiting at the new house with all of our worldly possessions, other than all the prune-stained stuff in the trunk of the car. When we got to the new house the first thing I did was fall down the stairs. It was all downhill from there. Something dreadful had happened to me. I was falling down the stairs and lisping. I didn't want to face it despite all the black and blue marks on my rear end. I had to support us with what was left of my business after Lou had lost his business. We had to survive. Little did I know that Lou hadn't paid the rent.

I'm sitting in my office downstairs at 6:00 am with packing tape stuck all over my pajamas. I hear some guy banging and pounding on the front door. "Marshal! Open up the door right now or we'll knock it down." It was like The Big Bad Wolf growling "I'll huff, and I'll puff until I blow your house down."

A huge muscular Marshal pushes through the door and screams "You have five minutes to evacuate the property!" *That wasn't even enough time to put on my makeup!* A locksmith that looked like Eddie Haskell on "Leave it to Beaver" rushes in and starts changing all the locks. (Who names their kid Beaver?) Only in the fifty's when there were no young boys running around with AK rifles shooting everybody. Can you imagine a mass murderer named Beaver? How times have changed, but even then, a beaver was a nickname for a female genital area. I never quite understood that. Vaginas don't build dams. Why don't they call it the Bermuda Triangle? Doesn't that make more sense? Anyway, I rush upstairs, wake up Lou, we grab a suitcase and throw in our medications, my makeup, throw on clothes, grab Lulu, our cell phones, and get into our sweat-lodge car. It was 118 degrees outside. *We were officially homeless.*

The main hotel here didn't have a room for us, so we ended up at the Hell Hole Hotel God knows what that "stuff" was leaking out of the bottom of the toilet. We sat on the bed, gathered our thoughts, and I got on my iPhone and started searching for another house to rent. We were fortunate to have several friends, God bless them, they lent us some money to start over again. It was a very scary time and we had zero security. Luckily, we worked as hard as we could and survived. *Failure was not an option.*

After the fiasco *(don't ask)* with the two-story house and Screw-Yu Property Management, we moved into a smaller one-story house. I started to feel normal again and resumed operating what was left of my business, but more s--t happened. Lou's hearing was going, so in December 2019, we go to the Veteran's Administration in North Las Vegas in order to get Lou some hearing aids. A week later I woke up feeling violently ill with a high temperature, soaking wet night sweats, nauseous, dizzy, short of breath, and unable to get out of bed. It was the virus from hell, but no one had heard of Covid-19 yet. A month or two later, still violently ill, I was watching the local news and the newscaster reports, "The first case of the Covid-19 in Nevada has been reported at the VA Hospital in North Las Vegas." I was there right at that time.

"Oh great, timing is everything in life," I said

jokingly to Lou, half-dead from my mystery virus. I don't really think you can be half dead; You're either dead or not dead. *But, whatever.*

In March of 2020, we're watching the local news and the newscaster reports, "The first Covid-19 patient has just died at the VA in North Las Vegas." I'm still feeling very sick, and now I may die too. I had lost forty-five pounds and my hair was falling out of my scalp like leaves falling off trees in fall. I went to the ER and told them I wasn't myself. *I don't know who else I thought I was.* They admitted me, gave me every test they could bill my medical insurance, and found older brain damage from a previous stroke and new brain damage from a TIA. My mind went from denial, to truth, to acceptance, to resilience. *I'm going to beat this thing! I'm going to show my body who's boss!*

Fast forward, I've been to almost every kind of doctor known to mankind except a proctologist, but that's only because I don't have a prostate gland. I've had every medical test that they've ever invented to torture patients and bill insurance. The infection disease doctor told me I had Long Covid but that there was no cure for it. I laughed. At least laughing didn't hurt. Life can be one problem after another. We solve one and the next one pops up. All we can do is try to solve each problem as it happens. It's just the way life is. I was stubborn and refused to let this illness stop me from doing anything. *Stubbornness* can be either bad or good. It can be a way of denying a life-changing truth, like cancer, and refusing to do anything about it and ending up dying. Or it can be a way of challenging a life-changing truth and making the best of it. In my case, my stubbornness gave me the strength to keep on trying to get better, save my business, and write this book.

CHAPTER TWELVE
Overcoming Fears That Make You Unhappy

F EARS ARE ONLY worries about what *can be* the worst thing that could happen to us. They are good in the sense that they are warning us to take action to protect ourselves from some horrible thing that *could* happen that we *can* control, like accidentally sticking a knife in the toaster and electrocuting ourselves. In order to age happily, we need to let go of the fears of events that *may* happen that we have no control over, like earthquakes, floods, hurricanes, and tornadoes. These are events that will probably never happen, but if they do, we can protect ourselves financially with insurance. We can fear a political catastrophe and World War III because they are possible, but as we age, we realize standing on street corners waving political signs or marching in demonstrations are usually fruitless and we could get arrested. We will be happier accepting this reality and just vote for who we deem the best candidate. If you fear an asteroid destroying earth or a complete drought, there is no insurance (I called our insurance broker) but don't worry, if that happens everyone will be dead. However, there are some events, like the sudden death of a loved one, a terminal disease, or being hit by a car that are fate, and there is usually nothing we could have done to prevent them. Worrying about your pure fate is useless because you have no control over it. Our fears can rob us of the joy of living, affect our health, and speed up our aging process.

Fear of Loneliness. As of the writing of this book, about 28% of older adults in the United States (13.8 million people) live alone according to a report by the Community Living's Administration on Aging of the U.S. Department of Health and Human Services. A study done by "Living Alone Over the Life Course: Cross-National Variations on an Emerging Issue," the number of elderly people who live alone ranges from 0 to 53 percent in the world. Loneliness leads to isolation, which increases the risk of dementia by fifty percent according to 2021 Consumer Affairs statistics. You're probably thinking, f--k the statistics, I'm really lonely. (Of course, if you already have dementia, you won't remember you're lonely.)

A client of mine was long-ago divorced, never remarried, and has lived alone most of her life confessed to me, "I'm so lonely I ache from the depths of my soul." I sympathize and empathize deeply with her. I know how much it hurts from just the short spurts of time I was alone. It was all-consuming and I felt like crying all the time. Aloneness is not a healthy way to live, especially as we grow older. We human beings have strong emotions and yearn for love.

We have an inborn calling to find a mate. All animals find mates, even birds like penguins and a few fish, like the French angelfish, find mates. *Do birds and fish date? Where are their sex organs?* It seems our Creator's intention was to have us enjoy sex in order to create offspring to populate the Planet Earth. Turkeys and chickens give birth without having sex and look what happens to them, they get eaten.

If you're a woman and can't find a mate one idea is to buy a vibrator, a jar opener, a trash compactor and hire a handyman for heavier jobs. It's smart to make a plumber your boyfriend or husband. You never know when you'll want to remodel your bathroom. If you're a man, it's a good idea to make a prostitute, a hairdresser, or a chef your girlfriend or wife. These relationships will save you a lot of money.

Seriously, the best idea to soothe the pain of your loneliness is to adopt a pet. Animals, especially dogs and cats, have a way of loving you like no human can. They will love you unconditionally and cuddle up with you as if you are the most wonderful person on earth. They are sad when you are sad and happy when you are happy. They will become your best friend. They don't argue with you. They aren't mean to you if you're kind to them. They aren't narcissists. (At least I don't think cats and dogs can be narcissists or sociopaths. *Maybe?)* The only downside is that they may pee and poop on the floor and humans don't (at least not polite humans).

Fear of Dementia. Forgetting where you parked your car in a large four-story parking lot is a lot worse than losing your mind completely, at least you know how to find where you parked your brain, which should be inside your head unless it escaped. Social isolation raises your chance of developing dementia. My mother and her sister, Aunty Dora, both developed Alzheimer's at the age of seventy. I had to put them in full-skilled nursing home until they died. (They never even recognized each other, which is a good thing because they always fought constantly.) I've always feared inheriting it, but so far, my brain is perfect and the damage from the strokes is gone. I believe that exercising my brain daily was and is the secret. Maybe I'll open a gym for brains with brain cycles, brain mills, and brain weights. I'll call it Brainercise.com. It will be open 24 hours a day for all of us older people with the curse of insomnia. If you want to stay youthful, and age happily and healthy, *always try to make negatives into positives.*

While some Alzheimer's is thought to be partially genetic, scientists at the Mayo Clinic are still testing it, but mild dementia is usually just age-related. The more we stay socially active, exercise our brains and bodies daily, and eat pure food instead of junk food, the better chance our minds and bodies will stay younger longer. Think young, think healthy, laugh a lot, and aging will become much happier for you! (I can't promise this though, I'm only human. It's up to you!)

Fear of the Loss of a Loved One. There are a lot of things that we lose as we get older, like our hair, perfect eyesight, cute figure, sexy six-pack abs, the names of things and people, keys, eyeglasses, mind, and the reason why we just walked into a room, but the most difficult thing to lose is a loved one. Nothing could be worse than losing a mate unless you really hated them and killed them, but going to prison for life and losing your freedom is probably quite bothersome. Maybe not, at least you get free meals and a roof over your head until you get raped or a shank or shiv in your back. I have been watching too many crime programs on TV. *(Forgive me, I digressed.)* Losing your child is the worst thing that could happen. I have clients that have lost their children. The empty holes in their hearts will never really heal. They're always thinking of how things should have been. I feel their sadness and help them accept what has happened and find ways to fill those holes.

It is only natural that we will lose our parents and other relatives as all of us grow older simultaneously. (I used to wish that everyone else would age and I would stay the same age, not this age of course, but when I was thirty-five. The problem would be that all my friends would be too old for me.)

Our country is so divided now that aging is the

only thing we can all do together. Maybe we should have aging parties and give each other canes and walkers as presents. It is always sad to lose people we love in our lives, but it is inevitable because we all play this game of life in sync. We have to keep on moving forward with our lives and learn to accept our lives without our loved ones. When we are able to move on, our lives will fill up with new relationships and experiences. We never know what tomorrow will bring. It's up to each of us to make good things happen no matter how old we are. Take positive action and positive things will happen. If you try to do something over and over again and keep on getting the same bad results, try something different. I learned that from Einstein, and he was pretty smart. If you want to stay young and be happy, *always move forward.*

Fear of the Loss of Dignity. As we were driving down the street the other day, I saw an old woman wearing filthy clothing, her skin severely wrinkled, and she had no teeth. She was trying to walk amongst the cars that were stopped for a red light and was holding a cardboard sign that I wasn't able to read. It was obvious that she was an alcoholic and/or a drug addict at the end of her life. I felt terrible for her. No human being should be so low that they have lost every ounce of their dignity. It hurt me deep down in my soul and I thought "there for the grace of God go I." I rolled down the window and gave her some money, knowing that she might spend it on drugs or alcohol, but not caring. I knew there was nothing I could do to save her at this point. I just wanted to know that she had enough money to buy some food and that someone cared. Compassion is necessary for loving yourself. If you're on Team Evil and have no compassion for others, please know that others will probably have no compassion for you.

Fear of abandonment is the main symptom of several mental disorders, most prevalent in borderline personality disorder (BPD). We all grow up believing that our friends and family will always be there for us when we get old and can't take care of ourselves anymore, but life is as predictable as a stoned weatherman. If we are married or have a life mate, or just a best friend, we assume they will always be there for us, but people die in accidents or from illnesses at any age, or they just decide they don't want to be with you anymore. Maybe you snore or grind your teeth or pass too much gas, who knows. If you have children, you probably assume they will take care of you when you're old, and hopefully they will. I did for my parents, but younger generations can have their own "issues" and some, not all, are more narcissistic than we were. Anything can happen. That's just life.

Years ago, Lou and I were moving to Beverly Hills because my daughter wanted to go to Beverly Hills High. They called it Beverly Hills High because all of the kids were "high." Lou, my daughter, Lou's daughter, and I were all going to be a happy family. I was going to prepare a nice home-cooked family dinner every night and we could all talk about our day. Don't ask me, "So how did that work out for you?"

Lou and I enjoyed laying at the pool watching the Beverly Hills cockroaches and rats from the alley diving into our swimming pool. It was really fun living without air conditioning in the hottest summers on record. We had to buy our own air conditioners, which consisted of water spray bottles and fans. It was fun to slide out of bed on our own sweat, kind of an inside Slip and Slide. I was going to make this work so my daughter could go to Beverly Hills High. We even had a Chinese houseboy, Joey, for a while. One day he brought his *whole family* to work with him to help. They were all dressed up in suits and dresses. His father opened the broom closet and pulled out the iron. "What dat?" he asked.

"It's a pancake press," I told him.

"Oh, *velly* good, I like *pancake*," he smiled.

I told my daughter, "You're going to live in this house we leased so you could go to Beverly Hills High and you're going to have dinner with us every night and we're going to be a family."

"F--k you, I'm going to go live with my father!" my teenager from hell screams as she storms into her room and starts screaming like a wounded hyena. I think the neighbors called the police but when the cops pulled up and heard her screaming, they got scared and drove off.

The next thing I know, Fart King pulls up in his two-seater Porsche convertible and she grabs as much of her stuff as she can, dumps it in the back of his car, jumps in and they drive off. I cried and felt terrible for a long time, and then I finally asked myself why anyone in their right minds would want to have teenagers and take this abuse. There should be a rental service called "Rent-a-Teenager." No one would ever want to have sex again.

I got into the bathtub for some alone time and turned on the Jacuzzi and cried, watching the washcloth getting sucked into the broken water jet, feeling like the washcloth being sucked deeper and deeper into the broken water jet as a metaphor for my life.

I talked to my daughter on the phone at her dad's house a few times after that and asked her "Why are you so angry about life?"

"Because my real mother abandoned me," she cried. I felt terrible, but little did I know that she had borderline personality disorder. Borderlines would rather abandon those closest to them for no reason rather than be abandoned by them, not that I would *ever* abandon my own child and she knew that.

"Do you want me to find your biological mother?" I asked nicely.

"Yes!" she screamed happily.

I remembered that her biological mother had wanted us to take her baby home from the hospital before she left the hospital so that she wouldn't feel like she was abandoning her baby, so I knew she was a caring person. There was only one thing to do. Find her biological mother and prove to my daughter that her birth mother loved her and wanted her to have the best home possible. *Boy, did I open a can of worms. It was a Wormathon.*

The next day I called the attorney who handled the adoption fourteen years prior, and he was able to find a Christmas card from the biological mother who still happened to live with her parents in another state.

Hesitantly, I dialed the phone. A little girl answered. I assumed this wasn't the mother unless the mother had given birth when she was one year old, so maybe she had another child.

"Is your mother home?" I asked.

"Oh my God!" the birth mother screamed, "Is she okay?" She innately knew I was the mother of her biological baby.

"Yes, yes, she's fine," I assured her.

I began to tell her the story of how she had gone to live with her father, and he had turned her against me to punish me for divorcing him. I felt like I was stepping over the line and pushing myself into her life and felt guilty. What I found out was that the little girl that answered the phone was my daughter's biological sister and that my daughter's birth mother had married, and since divorced, the biological father. We talked a lot after that and felt a connection. I really liked her, but the story took an interesting twist.

I called my daughter at her dad's house. "I found your biological mother!"

"Oh my God! Do I have any sisters or brothers?" she asked, intuitively knowing that she had a sibling.

I explained to her that her birth mother hadn't abandoned her, that she given her to a family that had enough money to give her a good life that she wasn't able to give her as a single mother with no money. When she found out that she was pregnant, she had gone to Los Angeles to stay with an uncle for the summer and never told anyone that she had given up a baby for adoption.

"Do you want to talk with them?" I asked my daughter.

"No, I'm not ready!" she said, crying.

I didn't know whether it was happiness or sadness. I understood how difficult it was and decided to let it be. ("Let it be" is usually a good decision for a lot of situations.) It wouldn't be until she was twenty-one that she would decide to contact her biological family. In the meantime, she wouldn't even talk to me.

Let's take a bullet train into reality, a place where we find the truth, which is that some people are not as kind and loving as we are. Most will do for themselves before they do for us. The real truth is that some of our children will think of us as a burden as we get too old to take care of ourselves. They have their own lives. Whether alone or with a family, we all need to stay as young and vital as we can so that we can take care of ourselves for as long as possible. Self-sufficiency and planning for the future helps lessen the fear of abandonment.

Fear of Loss of Security. Soon after my daughter had permanently stormed out of the house we had rented to make her happy, our landlord, Sergio, a sort of well-known Latino actor, suddenly kept on sending appraisers to our house all the time. I sensed something was cooking, but it wasn't me, I was on a cooking strike. What we didn't know was that Sergio was married to a former starlet in the Philippines who had been the lover of Fernando Marcos, the dictator of the Philippines who was married to Imelda Marcus, most famous for her closet full of 3000 pairs of designer shoes.

While we were living in the house, Sergio and his wife were charged with forty-two counts of bank fraud, bankruptcy fraud, selling millions of dollars of customized stolen cars to the Middle East, and making false statements in loan applications using bogus financial statements to obtain more than eighteen million in loans from at least thirteen financial institutions. They had concealed from the bankruptcy trustee numerous antiques, original paintings, and a Chinese ceramic collection, which were valued at more than six million in their financial statements. The indictment was one of the most massive cases of fraud against financial institutions in the history of Los Angeles.

The next thing we know is our front lawn is covered with news media and helicopters circling. The house we were living in was being auctioned off by the federal government and we had nowhere to go. Lou had made a deal with Ferdinand Marco's ex-lover (before she went to prison) to release us from our lease and return our security deposit if we let the public inside to see it in order to bid on it at the auction.

We left for the day and came home to every TV station in L.A. filming what was going on inside our house. (If I had known, I would have cleaned up a little better.) Mobs of would-be bidders were running all over our house. There was one kid standing on top of our big thick beveled glass dining room table tap dancing.

"Get him off our table!" I screamed at the father, as if it was okay for this swarthy character to have his kid tap dance on our dining room table.

"Go *f--k* yourself!" he screamed back defiantly.

"I'm calling the police!" I screamed back.

"Eat s--t!" the father screamed at me, grabbing his obnoxious kid off our table.

He was on "Team Bad". I already knew that continuing this would be bad for my mental and physical health, happiness, and wrinkles. All I learned from this was that *arguing with a person on Team Bad is a form of self-mutilation.*

Fear of Falling. Older people (older than what I don't know) fall often because as we age, our balance declines, we are wobbly, and our bones are more brittle and break easier than when we were young. I used to think that losing your balance is one of those things thought up by the companies that make canes and walkers, and pharmaceutical companies were putting drugs in Ensure to make us lose our balance and fall. The hip surgeons were in on the plot too.

As I was writing this book, we made our first

trip back to Los Angeles since the pandemic. It was Lou's major birthday and we stayed at our friend's house in a guest room above their garage. The stairs were steep and made of wood. By the time each of us had fallen three or more time down the stairs or on the floors in the house, the husband, a retired judge, says, "You two are going down like bowling pins!"

"I promise we won't sue," I said, still laying on their hard tile floor.

Falling is a big problem as we age because we can break our hips easily, so we need to hold onto railings, or we'll get down the stairs *really fast!* If we feel dizzy and our balance is off, we should use a cane. We can even decorate the cane and make it a fashion statement, like wrap it in red ribbon and make it a candy cane for Christmas. If you want to keep driving and feel you're up to it, great, but if you know your reactions are slower now and you're not as alert as you used to be, maybe it's better to use Uber, Lyft, or the driving service your medical insurance provides. The rideshare drivers are great as long as they've not been eating garlic or are drunk.

Fear of Death. We all worry about death more as we age. We fear that we will have to endure a lot of pain, but don't worry, there are drugs that can numb the pain. As our bodies are in the process of dying, our organs and brain start to shut down. We go into a dream state. Research suggests that even as our bodies transition into unconsciousness, it's possible that we can still be able to feel comforting touches from our loved ones and hear them speaking. Touch and hearing are the last senses to go when we die. Toward the end, we remain in this unconscious state of extended rest. If we want to enjoy our lives and be happy, healthy, and young we must accept that there is a beginning and an end to everything, even our lives.

I promised myself to stop myself from worrying about how many people are going to come to my funeral and what they're going to say at my memorial service. I now focus on how I see myself and what I can still do with my life to make the world a better and happier place. Who knows, there might not be anyone left that still loves me to give me a funeral or memorial service. The good thing about being dead is that this time you *really* don't care what people think about you anymore. The pressure is off. You don't need to be perfect anymore.

I have good news about *almost* dying. What I learned when I almost died from my first stroke is that my whole body felt very light, but I couldn't move it. It was the most peaceful I've ever felt. There was no pain. I didn't want to move as I lay in bed alone and looked at this beautiful light above me. I was mesmerized. It was like other people who have almost died describe it. I saw the light. This is why I no longer fear death, and you shouldn't either.

Dying fast in a car accident is a little different. I was with a friend, on the freeway using one of those driving apps and ended up in some deserted place where coyotes and mountain lions' roam. The app was *a little off* and instructed us to get off at a certain ramp, but as we approached the off ramp going 65 miles per hour there was a huge concrete barricade blocking it. We were a split second from hitting the concrete block. I screamed, and she quickly averted it, saving us both a trip to the morgue. Technology is terrific, *until it isn't.*

What I learned from *almost dying* fast is that if someone tells you that their whole life flashed in front of them, don't believe it unless they had shortest, most uneventful life of anyone in the world. I had a split second to live and the only thing I had time to do was scream.

Fear of Natural Catastrophes. If we turn on our television or surf the Internet, one station or website will be in denial about global warming and another station or website will be showing you videos of huge fires and flash floods with people standing on their roofs waving and screaming to be rescued by helicopters (if their roofs haven't been blown off or their house hasn't been flattened.) These videos make fear flush through our veins, kind of like iodine flushing through your body with a CT scan with contrast.

I was once in a hurricane and I had heard that the safest place to be in the bathtub, so I climbed into my bathtub. Nobody told me you weren't supposed to take off your clothes or fill up the bathtub with water. It was really embarrassing when the house blew away and the firemen came to rescue me.

It was January 17th, 1994, and the Northridge 6.7 magnitude earthquake woke us up at 4:30 am as we held onto our headboard for dear life. The furniture was sliding all over the room and the walls were cracking.

"Let's go out to lunch, I'm hungry," Lou declared in denial, as if the earthquake never happened.

"There's been a big earthquake, there's nothing open," I explain to him.

"You're overreacting as usual!" he gaslights me, trying to tell me I'm crazy.

We drove the streets of Santa Monica and all the car dealership roofs had collapsed and the cars were as flat as pancakes, the glass all broken, and the store alarms were all going off. As we got closer to Brentwood, there was no one in the streets, the stores and restaurants were all closed, every window on San Vicente Boulevard was broken, and we could hear a pin drop.

There wasn't a soul on the street, it was like "The Day the Earth Stood Still," but Lou wanted to have a nice lunch out.

Miraculously, we found this Chinese restaurant open in a courtyard under this large ten-story building. I explained to Lou that earthquakes have aftershocks, and it wasn't safe, but he was hungry. Unbelievably, there was this couple sitting alone at one of the tables having lunch and it was Norm, our State Farm Insurance broker, sitting there eating lunch with his young pretty girlfriend of the month. (This proves that "State Farm is always there for you.") We sat down and a Chinese waiter served us lunch. Shouldn't have Norm been talking to his clients, starting their insurance claims? And wouldn't you know it, my Chinese fortune cookie had no fortune inside of it again. *No fortune is better than bad fortune.*

We went to check on Sol, Lou's 96-year-old father, a widower who still lived alone still. When we got there, he was sitting in a living room chair, not noticing that every glass had fallen down from the glass shelves above the bar and that all the kitchen cabinets were open, and everything had fallen on the floor.

"Didn't you feel the earthquake, Sol? I asked.

"Huh?" he replied.

His hearing aids weren't working, and he didn't have a clue there was an earthquake. What I learned from this is "always keep your hearing aid batteries charged".

The earth is heating up fast and there are droughts and wildfires everywhere. Earthquakes are erupting as the temperature rises and dries up the soil. The oceans are heating up, causing all the hurricanes and tornadoes. The Covid pandemic is being ignored by many of us now, but we never know when the next variant will strike. The opioid pandemic and Fentanyl deaths are growing. There are wars breaking out all over the world and delusional young men mass murdering people with their illegal assault rifles. Worrying about things that you can do nothing about will keep you from enjoying your life. It will make you age faster and develop health problems.

So, what's to worry about? Just remember, if

earth is destroyed before we die, we'll be able to go to another planet, even if it has no gravity. Elon Musk is using SpaceX to eventually colonize the moon. Just think, if we live on a planet with no gravity, we will never need facelifts and breast lifts or need to worry about our balls hanging in the toilet, although I don't worry about the latter. I read that astrologists have discovered two new "Planet Killer" asteroids, but the good news is they won't hit Earth for many generations. *Do not fear that which you can't control.*

Fear of Flying. Flying gets harder as we age. First there is making the plane reservation for Hawaii on the Internet when you just finally learned how to do email. Next is packing your suitcases, stuffing in everything you own into just the two big cheap suitcases you got for free for signing up for AARP. (You never know what you'll need, so it's best to take everything.) Then you sit on your suitcases trying to zip them up and pull out your neck. Finally, you get the suitcases closed and your hernia pops out carrying those heavy free suitcases to the car. Hopefully you'll find a chiropractor and a general surgeon when you get to Hawaii.

You get on the freeway to go to the airport and there's a huge traffic jam. Once you get there, you spend another hour finding a parking spot in a lot that's not miles away from the terminal. The shuttle comes and you have to lug your luggage (Oh, that's why they call it luggage!) onto a shuttle with a drunk driver. Then you stand in the security line waiting half an hour until they get the obese person stuck in the walk-through X-ray machine out. Then you get felt up by a cute TSA agent (it's the best sex you've had in years) and pushed through another X-ray machine because the same TSA agent thinks you're carrying cocaine in your rectum, and you miss your flight.

You wait three hours for the next flight, however, your luggage got on your original flight, but you'll deal with that later. The new plane is a small plane with propellers and the pilot is asking everyone's weight before they board the plane. You just ate a whole pizza and a bag of donuts with a milkshake while you were waiting, so you refuse to give your weight to the pilot, and he refuses to let you board. You finally give in, and they try to figure out where they're going to seat you since they don't want the plane to be overweight and drop out of the sky. The flight attendant tells you if you want to fly, you're going to have to buy an extra seat. Okay, you buy an extra seat. *You shouldn't have eaten all that junk food.*

The guy behind you isn't wearing a mask and he's hacking away like he's got some new virus and the string on your only mask is broken. You settle in your seat and decide to enjoy the flight. The plane takes off, and they start playing loud rap music on the sound system. The flight attendant brings you hot coffee and spills it all over your lap. Now your genitals are burnt.

It's exciting, you finally see the lights of Las Vegas out the window, but unfortunately you were going to

Hawaii. The weather is hot, almost 120 degrees in Vegas, and the pilot has made two attempts to land, but it's really windy and the plane keeps on blowing off the runway. Each time the pilot tries to land they have to abort the landing and try again. (You should have eaten more junk food and added some French fries. That would have kept the plane from blowing off the runway.) Finally, the plane lands, but your luggage is in Hawaii *you think*.

Flying does have its hair-raising moments (unless you're completely bald). One time I was flying to San Francisco and our plane was just coming in full speed for a landing, the wheels were beginning to touch down, and suddenly the plane lifts back up in the air like at bat out of hell. *Are there bats in hell? No one wants to go down there and find out.*

"What's going on?" I asked the flight attendant.

"Oh, another plane was *just* coming in on the same runway," she explained nonchalantly.

Right after 9/11, I was flying to West Palm Beach and was seated across the aisle from this suspicious-looking man who kept on looking at his phone and then touching his shoes. *Aha! Another Shoe Bomber!* I told the flight attendant, who just graduated nursery school, about the man and she looked over at him, and then looked at me as if I belonged in a mental institution. *I was a little, well, er, a lot paranoid* after *9/11.*

I went back to my seat and pretended that I was air marshal disguised as a Jewish Princess and for five hours I kept giving him the evil eye every time he looked at his phone or bent down to touch his shoes. I felt it was my duty. To this day, I like to believe that he was a shoe bomber and I saved everyone in the plane. *Maybe I'm a hero.*

Another time I packed our suitcases way too quickly and kept on thinking what it was that I forgot. *Okay, so I was getting older. What was it?* We were on the plane from Seattle, Washington to Canada and when we were about to land in Vancouver, it finally came to me what I had forgotten. *Our passports!* Don't ask what we had to go through to get into Canada and then back through customs. We should have just walked over the border like all the other illegals, but I was wearing three-inch high heels, definitely the wrong kind of footwear to walk over a thousand miles to cross a border.

Fear of Being Attacked. All of us are afraid of being attacked at some time. One time I was walking in a parking lot at a mall and no one else was around. Suddenly, two gangbangers jumped out, one walking in front of me and one walking in back of me. *The red flags were waving at me.* They were laughing and obviously together. I sensed they were about to assault me, so I said loudly, "Oops, I forgot something!" and ran down the escalator quickly to get a security guard, who also looked like he would assault me. The two gangbangers were gone by the time the guard escorted me to my car. Maybe they had wanted to rape me, rob me, or hijack my car. Maybe they were harmless. It doesn't matter. We should always pay attention to the red flags. It is always better to err on the side of caution.

You can't say I'm not stupid. One night, in between my two marriages, I went with a girlfriend to a disco in Beverly Hills called The Candy Store, but they didn't sell candy. I was having a great time dancing. There were two guys there watching me all night. I thought I might have toilet paper on the bottom of my shoe. They were nice-looking guys, well-dressed, and affluent looking, so I figured they were harmless. *Wrong. Don't judge a book by its cover.* (Okay, so maybe my books.)

Towards the end of the night, one of them came over to me and asked me if I would like to join him and his friends for a late-night snack at Dino's on the Sunset Strip. "You can bring your friend, too" he offered.

I asked my friend if she'd like to go, but she said, "No, I'm really tired, but they're really nice guys. I know who they are. "You go ahead. They're fine."

The guy said he would drive me home after, so feeling a little hungry and wide awake, I decided to go with them. I went outside with them, and a parking valet pulled up in a brand new shiny red Corvette. I could see the personal license plate which said "ALL4ONE", but the real meaning didn't hit me until I was sitting on the middle console between these two guys, and I started to feel a *little* uncomfortable. The car took off and we were driving down Sunset Boulevard when I spotted a very stoned, disheveled girl with her thumb out. *Maybe she was just feeling for the air temperature or drying her nail polish. Who knows?*

The driver looked in the rear-view mirror and said to his friend. "They're still behind us and they picked up some stoned broad."

"Who's behind us?" I asked, getting really nervous.

"Just a few other guys that are coming with us to Dino's," he said as he continued driving and then went right past Dino's, which was closed.

"Dino's is closed!" I said in a panic. I knew something was wrong. "Let me out here. I'll call a cab." I was beginning to think this was kidnap.

"Don't worry," he said. "We'll just go to Oscars on top of the Holiday Inn in Hollywood. It's open all night."

They wouldn't let me out of the car and cell phones weren't invented yet. They kept driving and pulled into the parking lot of the Holiday Inn, along with the other guys in the car that was behind them and the scuzzy girl they had picked up. There must have been six or seven guys altogether now. *I was finally getting the drift of this situation.*

They took hold of both my arms tightly and dragged me out of the car into the empty lobby and then pulled me into an elevator. *Was I being too paranoid? Maybe this is okay?* I wanted to be optimistic, but I didn't want to stick around to find out. Then I noticed a poster on the elevator wall. It was an ad for Oscars. It closed at midnight. It was 1:00 am. *I was being kidnapped!*

Sometimes I'm not a quick thinker. They were all going to gang rape me. I remembered the license plate, "ALL4ONE". *How stupid had I been? Very!* I started screaming for help and yelling as loud as I could, tears pouring out of my eyes.

"We're just going to a room and order some food," one of them said, while the others were trying to pull me out of the elevator and down the hallway to a room. I knew it was too late for room service and I had lost my appetite anyway.

I kicked and hit and screamed and cried as hard as I could until one of them who had a heart saw that I wasn't that kind of girl, *er, woman*, grabbed me and got me into another elevator and drove me home. I never told anyone for a long time. I didn't even report it to the police. I was too embarrassed that I had been so stupid. At least I know that there were six or seven males that thought were willing to have sex with me. Again, every cloud has a silver lining. This is how I learned to know quickly spot people that are on Team Evil. If you want to stay young, healthy, and happy, you need to spot Team Evil quicker than I did. *Be cautious. Think about everything before you react.*

Unfortunately, the fear of being attacked is realistic. As we get older, criminals see us as weak and unable to defend ourselves. Try not to be or look vulnerable. Don't put yourself into dangerous situations. Carry a little canister of pepper spray or mace. Even take a self-defense class. Keep your phone in your hand in case you have to call for help. The more equipped you are to handle an attack, the less likely it is to happen. As we age, we don't have to look helpless.

CHAPTER THIRTEEN
When Life Gives You Cow Dung, Make Fertilizer

T HE *ACCIDENT.* LIFE hit me one day when I was twenty-one years old. I was cleaning the shower stall mold with bleach. (I was obsessed with winning over the mold in the shower. It was a war, the Invasion of The Green Slime.) My sister was getting married that night and I wanted the shower stall to be slime-less. *Like the shower stall was going to the wedding.* I have no idea why it was so important to me. I just hate mold. I even hate Jell-O molds. The phone rang. I answered it in my bleach-stained underwear and bra. It was Kaiser Permanente where my father had been a radiologist and had died just a few years prior.

My father's secretary was screaming hysterically into the phone, "Your mother's been in an accident, and you need to come to the hospital right away! Take a taxi!" she said. "Rush!"

By the time I got to the hospital, the doctors were all waiting for me before they wheeled my mother into surgery. She had driven her brand-new Buick Riviera off a six- hundred-foot cliff and landed on someone's garage below while driving down Nichols Canyon to get her hair done and pick up her dress for my sister's second wedding that night. They didn't expect her to live, but if she did, they were almost sure they would have to amputate one leg. *One's better than none, I guess. I wanted to be optimistic.* They had been waiting for me to get there to sign the consent form before they started the surgery. I was all alone with no one. I signed. I called my then husband, Fart King, and as a credit to him; he got there as fast as he could. I called my older sister to tell her about the bad accident and she told me she was going to go through with her wedding and was going on her honeymoon to Mexico. Never once did she call in to see if mother was alive or dead for two weeks. I learned that not everyone "does what is right", some just "do what is right for *themselves*."

My mother's surgery went as well as could be expected. Her arms and legs were both broken badly, and her jaw was wired shut, which was a blessing in this case. I felt terrible for her and spent every day with her in the hospital making sure they were taking good care of her. She seemed fine considering she couldn't move or eat and seemed to enjoy the attention she was getting in the hospital. Since my father had died, she was very lonely, now she was surrounded by doctors and nurses who paid a lot of attention to her.

The good news is that they saved her leg. I have no idea what ever happened to the Buick Riviera because it was totaled and towed away. For all I know it had faulty brakes and I should have sued. But I had too much on my plate to think about that. When my sister returned from her honeymoon, she stayed a week or two in L.A., divorced her newest husband, moved to New York, and found a third husband. I guess she just walks down the street and asks the first guy she sees "Hey, you want to get married?" and they say *"Sure."*

The Guns. After six months my mother was released from the hospital. I had to sell her home at the top of Nichols Canyon and move her to an apartment close to me. I hired a lovely middle-aged couple to help me pack up all her belongings and take care of the move to the new apartment I had found for her. Apparently, the people next door thought we were robbers, and the next thing I know I have two cops holding their guns to my head. I explained to them that I was moving my mother to a new apartment and told them the whole story, but they didn't believe me. They told me if I was the daughter, I had to find a photo of me in the house if I didn't want to get arrested and go to prison, or maybe even shot.

I spent forty-five minutes with two guns to my head (Why did they need two guns; wouldn't one gun have done the job?) looking through every drawer and cabinet until I finally found a small photo of myself. Apparently, my parents did think enough of me to put a framed photograph of me on display in their home. *This made me feel great.* So that was the beginning of taking care of my mother, getting her physical therapy, fed, bathed, finding her a new apartment, and whatever it took to do the right thing.

Alzheimer's. A few years after the accident my mother called me. She was crying and scared. "Rima, I don't know where I am!"

"Either do I," I teased.

"No, I'm really dizzy and confused," she slurred.

I rushed her to the emergency hospital. The doctor gave her tests right away. "It's "probably Alzheimer's disease," the doctor told me, although they didn't know how to diagnose Alzheimer's in those days without the patient being dead and doing an autopsy. That was not an option. I'd settle for plain-old dementia.

I made an appointment for her to see a neurologist in the next few days, but I couldn't let her live alone. She wanted to drive her car and slipped into the driver's seat when I took her home. "Which is the gas, and which is the brake?" she asked me.

I grabbed her keys and that was the end of that. I was able to get her to sign a Durable Power of Attorney for healthcare and finances, but I couldn't get her to go to an assisted living facility. The next morning, I got a call from the police.

"Your mother called us and said you were stealing all of her money," he told me.

I explained she had dementia and that I'm trying to get her into a home, but she won't go.

"I get it," the cop said. "Good luck. You need it."

The next morning, I get phone calls all day from my mother screaming "Drop dead you bastard daughter!" over and over again. It hurt me badly, but I knew she was mentally ill. I had been called a lot of names by now, but "bastard daughter" was a new one. (Maybe my mother was trying to tell me that I was born out of wedlock.) This went on for over a week, all day every day. I called one of these services that helps people with aging parents to place them in an assisted living facility. She was kicked out of the first assisted living home because she would strip down naked and walk around the facility all night. The service took care of it and got her into a fully skilled nursing home, and then charged us $500 a month just helping get her in a facility (not the facility itself) for the next eight years.

I was exhausted and I had my interior design business, my custom furniture rental business, my daughter, Lou's daughter, and Lou's dad, who was turning a hundred years old, to take care of. It was too much. My body couldn't take it and I was about to break.

The Pyromaniac. The quiet people above us in Pacific Palisades sold their condo. The new buyers were a Middle Eastern couple and their teenage son. No problem, they seemed nice enough. One day there was a big fire in the mountain above us. The woman upstairs was fearful of fires, so I took our her in my car to the top of the mountain to look at how far the fire was from us, which was just in the canyon across the street and up the hill a few blocks. She thanked me.

We suspected the fires were being set by this kid that lived right up the hill from us. He had even taken us to see his bedroom while we were at a party at his parents' house. The room was filled with tons of firefighting equipment, books, and pictures. He was obsessed with fire. He would even show up to all the fires he set in his little firefighting outfit. The fire department couldn't do anything about it because his father, an attorney, had threatened to sue the fire department if they accused his son, so we were destined to live very close to our neighborhood pyromaniac. I would have preferred living next to a nuclear reactor, it was safer.

The Terrorists Above. It wasn't long before the teenage son upstairs started going on rampages every day and night. He would throw things around the house and scream things in some foreign language. When he wasn't having rampages, he was sitting at his computer, probably planning something to ruin life in America as we knew it.

One day I was busy writing, and I heard these blood curdling screams coming from above us. The teenage son was throwing things, including a mattress, across the room. The next thing I hear are helicopters above with their loudspeakers blasting. I turned on the news and I watched it on the local news as it was actually happening above me. I think the kid was arrested and released because he was back upstairs the next day.

The night of 9/11, while the rest of the U.S. was mourning the loss of 6000 people that died in the Twin Towers, I hear our upstairs neighbors having a huge party, clapping, stomping and laughing and shouting things in a some other language, but I could understand enough to know that they were having a party celebrating the *success* of the terrorists that brought down the Twin Towers and thus must be terrorists and/or pro-terrorism themselves. Leave it to us to live in a condo with terrorists right over our heads. (First, it's Fernando Marcus connection, now it's Osama bin Laden.)

The next morning, I call the FBI and some doofus answers the phone as if he's taking my order for a large pizza with pepperoni and I tell him that we have terrorists living above us that are celebrating the success of 9/11. He took all the information and said the FBI would look into it. They never did. Apparently, he thought I was some nutcase and he crumbled up his notes and tossed them in the garbage. I wasn't prepared for what would come next. None of us are. *Until it happens.*

Fun in the Cancer Ward. A few months later, I was in the bathroom getting ready to take a friend out for her birthday lunch when I noticed blood in the toilet. I knew toilets didn't bleed, but I finished getting dressed and went ahead with my lunch date. When I got to my friend's office to pick her up, I felt so sick I wanted to die and excused myself to go to the bathroom, where my whole body emptied itself out and I was white as a sheet. I decided to try to get through her birthday lunch because I didn't want to cancel and I loved the food at Crustacean, so I went and just mentioned to my friend about the bleeding.

"Oh, it's probably a little bladder infection," she said, trying to make light of it, or maybe just wanting to finish her free lunch. "Just go to your gynecologist and he'll take a test."

After lunch, I sped over to my gynecologist's office. I knew something was wrong, really wrong. I was very sick. He gave me a urine test and told me that I didn't have a urine infection. By then I was trying to stop myself from passing out.

I drove over to my internist's office, and he sent me over to a urologist's office just to appease me. I had my hair and nails and makeup all on, so, like all doctors, they think I'm neurotic and that there's nothing really wrong with me. (Now I try to look like I've been sleeping in my car for months, so they'll listen to me.)

The urologist gave me a cystoscopy and there was definitely blood in my bladder. He sends me right over to have a CT scan.

I drove over to the radiology lab to get a CT scan. They kept me on the table a long time after the scan, left the room to call my doctor, and came back to give me another scan with dye. It was on a late Friday afternoon, so they told me to go home, and that the urologist would call me on Monday. It was a very long weekend.

Monday morning the urologist called and said, "Come into my office immediately!"

"I know it's bad news," so I said "Please tell me now. I don't want to wait for the truth."

"It's bladder cancer," he said. "You have a high-grade tumor in your ureter. Come in right now and we'll discuss what we must do immediately."

I was stunned. My facelift dropped down to my boob job and my boobs were now resting on my thighs, which was good because my thighs were shaking, and my boobs comforted them. When I got to the urologist's office with Lou, the urologist says to me, "You need to find a urologic surgeon who specializes in high-grade ureteral surgery immediately." I needed time to absorb what was happening to me and to find the right surgeon. Cancer is for other people, not me. We all think it's not going to happen to us and are shocked when it does.

The first urologist/surgeon wanted to take out the tumor laparoscopically and insisted I would need chemotherapy. The next doctor wanted to do the same, only remove a big part of my bladder. I liked my bladder; I didn't want to walk around with a urine bag for the rest of my life; I liked to wear tight jeans. The next urology surgeon, Dr. Jerk, put my CT scan up on his lightbox upside down.

"Is that the tumor?" he asks, pointing to my pelvic kidney.

"Nope, that's my kidney" I say. I did have one kidney in my pelvic area, God knows how it got there, maybe it walked, but Dr. Jerk should have been able to figure it out.

"Oops" he says, "I've got your x-ray upside down. He turns the x-ray right side up.

"Oh! There's the tumor!" he said proudly.

He told me that chemotherapy was absolutely necessary. I was out the door quicker than a dinner guest that had eaten my best friend's vegetable casserole. If he couldn't find the tumor on an x-ray, he certainly wasn't going to find it in my body.

Doctor Jerk called me the next day and he sounded very mad and agitated. "*Ma'am*, when are you going to schedule your surgery with me?!" I dislike (well, I admit hate) when someone calls me "*Ma'am*" more than I hate when someone sends me an email that starts off with "*Hey.*"

"Never" I replied and hung up the phone.

Yes, I know if we want to be happy, we have to eliminate the word "hate" from our vocabulary, but I'm not perfect. Perfection is never achievable. Let perfection go and you'll be happier and laugh more at your own flaws. I knew I had to avoid chemotherapy, if at all possible, because of what happened to the man who lived right next door to us, Bill Hootkins, an actor most famous for playing Sir Alfred Hitchcock in the play "Hitchcock Blonde." He had been fighting cancer and had a major stroke from all the chemotherapy and died soon after.

Five weeks had passed, and my situation was dire. I was told by all the doctors that if I didn't have surgery right away the cancer would spread quickly.

That night I got a call from a girlfriend whose husband coincidentally plays golf with a famous urologic surgeon who has a new method of operating on ureter cancer. People came from all over the world to have them operate on them. *There are no coincidences, but rather opportunities out Guiding Spirit brings us to keep us safe.* Dr. Skinner actually called me that night and told me to get into his office at Norris Cancer Center with my CT scan and x-rays the next morning.

Alone, I pulled up to the building and the sign read Norris Cancer Center. I started to cry. *Cancer.* It was real. I had cancer. This was happening. It wasn't a bad dream. Dr. Skinner took me immediately, showed me the large dark tumor on the CT scan I had brought him, told me it was high-grade, and explained his surgery. He was going to remove the complete ureter with the tumor in it and replace it with a piece of my intestines and then hook it back up to my bladder. He sounded like he was a plumber that that was going to remodel my kitchen with used copper plumbing. He told me that I may or may or may not need chemotherapy, so at least there was a chance that I wouldn't need it, but the scar would be very large since they had to open up the whole trunk of my whole body. He had already scheduled my surgery for the following day. I had no choice if I didn't want to die. Too much time had elapsed.

The surgery took about ten hours, and I woke up in the cancer ward with tubes and IV's hanging out of me and in severe pain. *Cancer ward, me?* I cried as I looked down at the slit in my body that went from my crotch up the middle of my body to under my boob and across to my right side, almost four feet long. (I'm tall.) I felt like I was a Snickers bar that had been unwrapped and slit in two pieces with a tube draining all the caramel filling out of me.

Norris Cancer Center was a teaching hospital, so Dr. Skinner loved to bring his entourage of good-looking young male students to my room at about 6:00 am each morning and explain my case to them. I would wake up every morning for two weeks looking up to a bunch of young, cute medical students staring up at me and would start laughing and they would too. One morning I had got myself to the bathroom and Dr. Skinner and his entourage had come in and opened the bathroom door to find me sitting on the toilet. They were all laughing. I laughed too. What else could I do? *Laughter is healing.*

After two weeks in the cancer ward Dr. Skinner walked in with good news. The doctors at Norris had their meeting about my case and the biopsies of other tissues were in, and the cancer had been encapsulated. I didn't need chemotherapy. I would just need to have a cystoscopy every six months for five years. (As of the writing of this book, it's been over 20 years and I've been cancer free! My Guiding Spirit has been watching over me. *We all have a Guiding Spirit watching over us.*

The whole trunk of my body looked like a map of the Mississippi River, but I was alive albeit no more walking around naked in the health club locker room.

I eventually continued on with my interior design business, but life kept on throwing whammies at me and still does. *I wasn't going to let anything stop me! Neither should you!*

The Incredible Disappearing Street. Here come more helicopters again. I'm minding my own business in my bathroom getting dressed to go to an appointment, watching the TV, and I see something happening on the local news and watch as helicopters swarm around a huge sinkhole in the Palisades Highlands. It piqued my interest because it looked like it was right where we were living and there were helicopters circling right over our townhouse. *I put two and two together.*

I go outside and walk to the edge of our driveway, which was once our sidewalk and street, and there's this humongous sinkhole right in front of our driveway stretching from blocks down the hill to blocks above the hill. The news media was swarming all over the place and trying to interview me as if I really knew what was happening, but of course I had no clue why our whole street had disappeared. I had wet hair, no makeup, and was wearing a bathrobe and slippers. I had no intention of making this my TV debut, so I ran back into our condo praying that no one had caught a shot of me in my bathrobe and wet hair. I am not exactly a natural beauty. It takes a lot of time, work, and sleight of hand.

The Crash. In 2008 the stock market and real estate crash happened, my interior designer business was dead, Lou had to close his auto salvage business, the value of our house went down fifty percent. We couldn't pay the mortgage, HOA dues, or property taxes after paying all my medical bills and our parents' nursing home bills, and we were getting foreclosure notices on our home of twenty years. I had to sell *everything* I had on eBay, including my diamond wedding ring. I wrote and published my book "Choose to Be Happy: A Guide to Total Happiness" to pay some of our expenses. *Resilience* is my middle name and *happiness for everyone* is my goal in life.

Some of our wealthy friends had lost everything too. They started giving me all their designer bags and stuff to sell on eBay, and this is how I accidentally started my online business, Authentic Designer Stuff, which blossomed into seven online stores, but we were still just making ends meet and our house was still going into foreclosure. Living on the Westside of Los Angeles was too expensive and our savings, checking, and brokerage accounts were running on empty still and then a miracle happened. *My Guiding Spirit appeared again.*

The Miracle. I was opening the mail and I saw this envelope offering us a decent amount of money to short sell our house. I thought it was a scam and I started to throw it away but saw it was from our mortgage bank, so I opened it up. We decided to take the money, short sell our home of twenty years, accept losing our house that we could no longer afford, and took a lease on a house in Encino, which was more affordable. The problem was …

The Newest Neighbors Upstairs. Here comes more cow dung. The terrorists had moved out and a new, older couple with grandchildren (lots of them) had moved in upstairs. The grandchildren would scream, yell, and jump up and down as loudly as they could whenever they visited, which was every day. Her husband had just died, so I didn't want to bother her about it. One day I ran into her and told her that we were forced to short sell our house at its current value, which was almost fifty percent lower than what it had been at the top of the market. I could see the darts fly out of her eyes at me as she smiled. We were *forced* to sell our condo now at a low price and it would affect the value of her condo for a while.

On the first Sunday our broker held an Open House. The upstairs neighbor's son brought over every one of his children and their friends, all one hundred of them. He instructed them all to jump up and down and scream and yell and make as much noise as they could during the entire Open House. I was livid, so I called upstairs, and the son answered the phone.

"Hi, it's Rima downstairs, can you please keep your children quiet please? We're having an Open House," I asked politely.

"Go f--k yourself! Go to a hotel if you don't like it!" her lovely son screamed into the phone. *Cow dung can get really smelly.*

Our condo finally sold, but for a lot less. What I learned from this experience is that some people are just mean and nasty. They are on Team Evil. Don't give them the power to poison your happiness. Just move on if you can. If you can't move on for a valid reason, find professional help. (That doesn't mean a hitman!)

Fires, Naked Men, and More Terrorists. The house we leased Encino was great except for the hot 100-degree summer weather and the wildfires burning around us all the time. I needed a gas mask to walk outside. One day I was working in my office and this naked man climbed over our locked gate and ran past my office. I thought I was hallucinating. He tried to open the glass sliding doors, but they were locked, so he runs around the side and starts banging and screaming to get in through the laundry room door. I knew he didn't have a gun or knife since he was naked. We called the police, but he ran. Maybe our next-door neighbors would enjoy seeing his schlong more than we did. Such is my life as a nutcase magnet. I've learned to laugh at it.

There was a huge house right above us on a private road. We used to hear huge parties there. Several times the police came with helicopters blaring loudspeakers ordering the parties to disburse. One night we were watching the terrorist attack in France on the news. We could hear a huge party at the same house, and everyone was laughing and clapping and screaming "Die Israel, Die! Leave it to us to lease *yet another* house right next to terrorists.

I called the FBI once again and got pretty much the same response about it as I did about the terrorists at our condo in the Palisades. The FBI operator told me that the FBI would look into it. When the FBI goes on TV and tells everyone to report everything they see, it's a ploy. They just want to hear the phone ring, so it looks like they're busy. What I learned from this experience was that we're all on our own when it comes to push and shove. I have learned not to let the incompetence of others and a no-win situation destroy my happiness. *Let it go.*

The cow dung kept coming. After the 2016 election, my online sales started dwindling because the dollar was very strong, and seventy-five percent of my sales were international. I had a stroke that I didn't know was a stroke and kept on operating my slowing business. By 2018, we decided to move to Las Vegas because we could live much cheaper, and we could survive. Staying young and happy forever requires *fortitude.*

CHAPTER FOURTEEN
Are You the Hamburger Generation?

H AVE YOU EVER wondered what it would feel like to be a hamburger? *Probably not.* As we age, everyone else ages too. If you've gone to a high school reunion you've figured this one out. If you can make it to middle age, you may become part of the Hamburger Generation. I have several clients like this that suffer from bun-burden. The bun is our mate. The patty is our children or grandchildren. The cheese is our aging parents. The lettuce is our aging relatives. The onions are our siblings. Ketchup is our career. The cardboard box it comes in is our house, which is a mess, and the side of French fries are our friends and dinner guests. The sweet pickle relish smeared inside the hamburger is *us*.

The Bun: Your Mate. Time went on and Fart King (remember him) wanted to have a baby (well, not Fart King himself, he didn't have a uterus, just a penis. I know that because he used to hang his underwear on it and parade around the house.) Having a baby was the thing to do in those days, like burning your bra, wearing hippy clothes and letting your hair grow long. I stopped taking birth control pills but never got pregnant. I surmised that this was because we rarely had sex, but I would be proven wrong late in life. In any case, we went through all kinds of fertility tests and would have sex when I was ovulating, and I would lie in bed with my legs up in the air for two hours looking like an open pair of scissors waiting to be sharpened. *Nada. Nothing.* I took pills, I had painful endoscopies, and I spread my legs for the gynecologist with his big shaggy dog in his office barking at my crotch more times than I want to admit, but I never got pregnant.

We decided to adopt, but there were very few babies to adopt at that time and the waiting list to adopt a baby was three to four years. There was an attorney that handled adoptions in one of Fart King's buildings that he managed. He found us two babies that were due to be born soon and gave us our choice of adopting the baby of a Go-Go dancer who was very short with blonde hair or the baby of a very religious Catholic woman who had come to L.A. to have her baby so she could keep her pregnancy a secret from her family. She was tall with brown hair, a better physical match for us. We did know that physical attributes were genetic, but no one in those days told us that mental conditions could be genetic too, so we didn't ask.

When the baby was born, we rushed to the hospital to see our baby girl in the nursery. Her little head looked like the doctor had taken her out of the birth mother's womb with a pair of BBQ tongs. Fart King had never seen a newborn baby before and insisted the baby was deformed. He made our new pediatrician rush to the hospital immediately to examine the baby. Luckily, she was perfect.

Three days later we were told to come to the hospital with one receiving blanket, signed all the papers, paid the bill, and a nurse just handed us our baby. The nurse told us, "Please leave the hospital with your new baby before the mother leaves the hospital." (Is there such a thing as an old baby?) This was our clue from this that the biological mother wanted to make sure her baby was going to a nice home and would have a good life. We were in heaven. Now I was part of the park group in Beverly Hills with all my girlfriends who had just had babies. Life was good. *Until it wasn't.*

Things changed. Fart King would take our daughter out all day on a "date" in her baby carrier while I stayed home, cleaned the house, and washed dirty laundry. He would take off his clothes at night and drop his dirty underwear, socks, and whatever ugly outfit he was wearing that he knew I hated on the floor. I was his poor slave who picked it up, washed and folded it, and put it neatly away. That's what *I thought* good little wives did in those days.

If I didn't put away something exactly perfect, he would get mad and say, "Don't confuse efforts with results."

So, when he couldn't get it up, I'd say to him "Don't confuse efforts with results."

Fart King's obsession with our baby was so far out that he used to climb into her crib, which was quite a feat since he was 6'4" tall. Secretly I prayed he would get stuck in there. He would take her on his motorcycle, with no helmet, for short rides. I screamed at him not to do it, but he wouldn't listen. There were other weird things that he did. A part of me knew a part of their relationship was a little sick, as was ours, but I didn't know what to do. I was only twenty-five years old and had no guidance. When I had gone to my parents right after I married him and realized I had made a mistake, they told me, "You made your bed, you lie in it" and I was afraid to tell any of my friends about all this. I was abused by my husband and felt deeply unhappy all the time. I felt stuck. I wanted to commit suicide. Instead, I found my power of self that was hidden deep inside my soul and made it my mission to find joy again. What I learned from climbing out of this deep unhappiness was that it is always possible for any of us to reclaim our happiness no matter what happens to us and how old we are.

A few years later Fart King wanted to adopt another baby. I reluctantly agreed and started calling every adoption agency, and every attorney that dealt in adoptions. Finally, I found one that was going to be born in a few months and he was to be ours. We named him Bryan and we redecorated the nursery for a boy, bought a whole new blue layette, and waited for our new son to be born. I wrongly thought that maybe a second child would cure my unhappiness, but I had a sick feeling in my stomach that something would go wrong. That sick feeling was my *intuition*. I trust my intuition more than I trust anything and I have learned to go with it. If you feel you have a strong intuition, start listening to it. *I believe our intuition is our Guiding Spirit watching over us.*

The attorney called us that night to announce that our baby had just been born. Instant baby, kind of like an automat in New York, just lift up the little glass door and pull out your little baby, no pregnancy, no trimesters, no getting fat, no labor pains, just an instant baby in a blanket. *It wasn't born in a blanket. We had to bring one with us.* We rushed to the hospital to see Bryan.

Later that night we got a call from the attorney. "There's a problem," he said solemnly. "The baby has some physical problems, and he will need several operations."

"Not a problem, we'll take care of it. We still want him," blurted out Fart King, ignoring me and my thoughts as if I was an outsider to this whole situation.

"Okay," said the attorney. "I'll draw up the papers. Come to my office tomorrow and sign them and Bryan is yours." We went to the hospital in the morning to see Bryan, and then went to the attorney's office to sign the papers. We just had to wait three days to pick Bryan up.

The next morning, we got a phone call from the attorney. "The good news is that Bryan is going to be okay, and he doesn't need the operations. The bad news is that the biological mother has decided to keep him."

Fart King cried. I was sad but realized that life works in strange ways. We may never know or understand the reason why things happen the way they do, but if we want to be happy, we have to accept what life throws our way. As we age, we need to realize that if things are meant to be, they will happen easily. If they are not meant to be, they will always be a struggle. If we accept that life works this way, everything is much easier to accept, no matter what happens to us. Everything happens for a reason. Your Guiding Spirit will reveal that reason to you when the time is right.

Next, Fart King brings home this Irish setter puppy for our daughter. Shandy grew to be about a hundred pounds in no time. Fart King would lock Shandy outside when he got too rambunctious, but he'd jump right through the glass doors (the dog, not Fart King), shattering glass all over like a Hippopotamus breaking into Leicester Museum & Art Gallery, which is filled with Picasso ceramics, although our house was filled with garage sale ceramics.

One day Fart King got so upset that he took Shandy and threw him out the back door and broke his leg. I was crying and screaming at him as the poor puppy was wailing in pain all the way to the veterinarian. I've always loved animals and knew that abusing animals was the sign of a potential murder. I tried to tell myself that he didn't mean it, that it was an accident. I was wrong. Several years earlier he had thrown our beautiful white fluffy cat out the balcony of our two-story apartment when she was in heat. I was upset and furious, but I was even younger and overlooked it. Fluffy came home the next day with a hangover. The next thing I know, I'm a feline midwife in the closet with Fluffy helping her give birth to eight beautiful little white fluffy kittens that were roaming all over our house.

I remember that the night after the Texas Tower mass shooting in 1966 when Charles Whitman, a student, an ex-Marine, fired down from the University of Texas clock tower, killing fourteen people, and wounding thirty-one people, Fart King said to me "I'd like to kill people like that someday." I was very young and remember thinking, "*Did I marry a potential mass murderer? What was I going to do? Whom could I tell? When was I going to be happy?*"

Fart King could be very nice and charismatic to other people, kind of like Ted Bundy. He would pick up characters off the street and invite them to dinner without letting me know and then he would show up two or three hours after they arrived.

Sometimes we put up with Team Evil people because we don't realize how degrading they are. Controlling people try to gaslight us into believing that we are stupid or crazy until we start believing it and render ourselves unworthy of being treated with the kindness and respect we all deserve. Once you open your eyes and realize that you deserve to be treated better, that being controlled by another person is toxic to your happiness, you will find your youth and joy again.

The Side of French Fries: Your Friends and Dinner Guests. One night the doorbell rang unexpectedly. I opened the door and these two huge muscular Mafioso characters in dirty white tee shirts looking like poor excuses for Mafia hit men are standing there. I was so scared Fart King had put a hit on me.

"Your husband invited us to dinner tonight," one says.

'*Yeh,*" the other one says gruffly.

I had no idea what strip joint Fart King picked them up at, but I was scared to death and had to cautiously entertain them for three hours until Fart King showed up, then cook dinner for us all. I humored them. I think their names were Nuncio and Rico, at least that's what I guessed. Other times he would invite weird tenants from his building. One time the Ambassador of Mexico and his wife showed up unexpectantly and I had to entertain them for two hours pretending to be a Jackie Kennedy in a dirty housedress until Fart King got home.

Another time he picked up a couple at the Beverly Glen art fair, invited them for dinner that night. The second dinner was over, he left and went to a movie with his friend. I am now quite sure that it really wasn't a movie they went to every Sunday night like clockwork. The word "cheater" comes to mind.

The Heist. One Saturday night I gave a dinner party for a lot of people and Fart King kept on inviting more and more people. Our dining room was filled with twenty or thirty friends, and they were all having a good time. One of the women went into the den to get something out of her purse where all the bags were placed. She screamed as she saw two men climbing out of our den window with all the purses. I had tried to tell Fart King we needed locks on the windows or doors. He had defied my good sense, an act I understand now was a way of demeaning me.

Everyone jumped up from the table and ran out the front door, screaming "Stop! Stop!" as they ran after the two burglars, which they never caught. After giving up and getting over the shock, we all had dessert, and everyone jokingly and forevermore accused us of staging the burglary as entertainment. It wasn't. The lesson here is to never live in a house in which no windows or doors have any locks. And don't marry an A-Hole.

It was the hippy days. Fart King had grown long hair and beard and his friend, Hippy Harry, had grown a Caucasian afro. They decided to go to Big Sur without us wives. *I wonder why.* Fart King put on the ugly brown cheap suede fringed jacket he had bought in Tijuana. I told him I hated the jacket, so he bought one in every color. He looked like he lived in a hippie commune, maybe with the Manson Gang.

179

Fart King and Hippy Harry, his sidekick, hooked their motorcycles to the back of our Cadillac and drove almost all the way into Big Sur. When they got there, they hid the Cadillac, got on their motorcycles, and rode into Big Sur as if they were Peter Fonda and Dennis Hopper in "Easy Rider." Fart King with his long hair and beard held down with a bandana, and Hippy harry with his Caucasian Afro and biker's boots. There is only one word to describe them. I think the word is "putz's". Don't marry a "putz" either. They couldn't even remember where they hid the Cadillac.

Well, if they could pretend they were Peter Fonda and Dennis Hopper in "Easy Rider," I could pretend to be "Nancy Sinatra in These Boots Were Made for Walkin'." My friend stuffed me into her size two hot pants, and I put on my high heeled boots, and we went to a disco in the Valley called The Point After. ("After what" I don't know.) I danced all night, and a lion tamer attacked me on the dance floor. *I swear.* This is when I realized I could enjoy life without Fart King. I felt free.

The two putzes finally found where they parked the Cadillac and made it back home unfortunately. Fart King and I go to see the movie "Bob and Carol, Ted and Alice." When we got home, Fart King he looked into my eyes and said, "I want to have an open marriage."

I looked into his eyes and said, "I want a divorce, so you'll need to move out of the house."

I was tired of his dirty underwear and socks on

the floor and rolled-up boogers on his nightstand. I was tired of his lies and cheating. My tolerance had gone out the door with my sex drive. He cried like a baby and spent the rest of his life punishing me by turning my daughter against me. We were officially separated, but Fart King wouldn't leave the house, so I told him he had to babysit. He did. Sometimes it's just time to say *"Enough!"* It had taken ten years.

The Beef Patty: Our Children and Grandchildren. Most people are naïve when they're young and want to have children. Babies are so cute. So are puppies, and they don't turn into teenagers. If you are lucky, your children bring you much joy and light up your life. You can learn a lot from your children and grandchildren by watching the joy on their faces as they learn and see the world through young eyes. You can relive your childhood with them by taking them to see new places, try new things, and just watch them grow up to be happy, well-adjusted adults. If you are *really* lucky, you will really enjoy being with your children and grandchildren and spend lots of quality time all with them. Lest we forget, babies grow up to be people with their own personalities and flaws. Sometimes not the ones we signed up for. And babies come with a "no-return policy."

The Cheese: Our Aging Parents. Aging parents are our responsibility. They took care of us when we were growing up, even put up with us when we were teenagers and did everything for us, so it is our responsibility to make sure they are taken care of as they age, like it or not. It is our obligation to treat them with the kindness and respect they deserve even if they weren't perfect parents. Parents have flaws, just like all human beings, and, in most cases, our parents did the best they knew how to do given the tools they had. Let's hope your children take care of you in the same loving way you took care of your parents. That doesn't always happen.

When Lou's father, Sol, was ninety-six years old and we were taking care of him, Lou's cousin, Sarah Sleazeball, edged herself into Sol's life and started taking him shopping and to the barber and places like that once a week. We thought it was so sweet of her, so we took Sol and Cousin Sleazeball out to dinner one night and she kept on rubbing his arm and telling us, "I love my Uncle Sol so much." That's so sweet, so we thought. *Wait and see.*

One day Sol, who was still driving (don't ask) had a car accident and hit his head. Sarah Sleazeball called us to tell us about the accident and we rushed right over to his condo.

"He's fine," Cousin Sleazeball assured us, "Just bumped his head a little."

"I'm fine," Sol told us as he lost his balance and fell on the floor.

We rushed him over to the emergency room. The neurosurgeon in the ER diagnosed a brain aneurysm and told us he needed immediate brain surgery. As they rushed him into the operating room he said to me, "Rima, don't worry about me. I've had a wonderful life." I cried. He was the sweetest man and thank God he did survive and was fine. It wasn't his time yet. Sol loved his life and was always sitting in his recliner chair laughing at old "I Love Lucy" episodes over and over again. He loved to laugh, which is why he probably lived to be 106 years old. I've always made sure I fall asleep for the night laughing. I try to watch late-night TV shows and listen to comedy monologues. If we can all spend what might be the final days of life saying "Don't worry about me. I've had a wonderful life," we will be successful. *Always try to go to sleep laughing. Never go to sleep angry. You will stay young and happy forever.*

One night we took Sol to his favorite restaurant, a deli, for corned beef on rye, the health food of his generation. Sol says to me, "Sarah is so sweet. She took me to see some man in this building to sign some papers." My ears perked up like a German Shepard sniffing a Chihuahua in heat, so I went home and started playing Sherlock Holmes.

Red Alert! Sarah Sleazeball had a relative by marriage who was an attorney, Sammy Scumbag, and she had changed Sol's will so that his condo and whatever money he had left would go to her. We needed his condo and money to keep him well-taken care of and we weren't going to let her get away with this. He was ninety-six years old but had brothers that had lived to be 106. I went into action and threatened her and her nefarious son-in-law with fraud and elder abuse and made Sammy Scumbag change back Sol's will. I was on alert for the next trick. *It happened.*

A few days later we took Sol to lunch again. He smiled and told me, "Sarah and her son-in-law are so sweet. They came by last night with some woman and took me in the car to sign some more papers. It was so nice of them."

"Sweet" Cousin Sarah Sleazeball couldn't change Sol's will anymore, so she had her attorney draw up papers that transferred Sol's condo, checking account, stock brokerage account over to her. She had tricked Sol into signing new documents transferring everything he owned to her and had already emptied out his account, so now she had all his money and owned his condo. Team Evil had attacked. I went into action! We must never let Team Evil win!

Coincidentally, her son-in-law was a stockbroker at the same office as my stockbroker in Century City. We rushed over to see the President of the company and threatened to sue him, the company, Sarah Scumbag, and her slimy son-in-law for fraud and elder abuse. We got it handled immediately and everything was transferred back to Sol. What I learned from this experience is that if someone is sickening sweet to you, they've got a card or two up their sleeve. *Beware! Especially of long-lost relatives when they smell money they can steal.*

We immediately filed for Durable Power of Attorney over Sol's heath care and money and hired a live-in caretaker. The agency told us they were sending over this wonderful woman who loved to cook. It sounded great. When she got there, she handed us a shopping list of ingredients that she wanted us to buy for her. When we got back with the groceries, Sol said he didn't like her. He wanted us to get rid of her. When we got there the next day to fire her, she was gone, as was all of his silverware, dishes, jewelry, knickknacks, and whatever else she could carry out. Well, at least there were a lot of groceries left, if you like Spam and jalapeno peppers.

Caretaker number two was a very pretty young girl, Barbara, in her twenties. She was sweet and took Sol places every day and he was in heaven. He thought these caretakers were staying at his house to take care of him for free. We didn't have the heart to tell that nobody was that nice.

Barbara stayed quite a while and one night we took them to dinner. Barbara confessed that she was really "sort-of" married in her own country, *but* when she and Sol went out together everyone thought they were boyfriend and girlfriend and that they had fallen in love. Sol was the love of her life. *Right. Could they have had sex together? It's a possibility.*

I told her, "This is such a wonderful love story. You do know that this condo doesn't belong to him, and he doesn't have any money, right?"

She just looked at me in horror.

We went over the next morning and found out that Barbara had picked up her belongings, left the love of her life alone to fend for himself. She was long gone.

Sol asked me, "Where did Barbara go?"

I told him, "She took a vacation to hell," I said.

"Oh," said Sol, "I hope she comes back soon."

"Sure, but it's a long elevator ride up," I told him.

Caretaker number three was a young man who

had the personality of a banana, but seemed kind and took good care of Sol. He lasted a good amount of time, until we discovered his cocaine hidden in Sol's closet. We didn't think Sol was snorting cocaine, so that was the end of that. We were out of patience and money for caretakers, and it was time to sell Sol's condominium and put him in a nice, assisted living facility. This did not make him happy, to say the least. *Don't ask.*

I know I sound cynical, but I've learned to never trust anybody unless they have proven that they are honest, sincere, and trustworthy. I know it's not a good way to live, but it's necessary in this upside-down world. I would rather have us all believe that all people are good, but that's not true. There will always be Team Good and Team Evil. If we want to stay young and happy—*and safe*, we have to accept the truth about mankind.

The Lettuce: Your Other Aging Relatives. I got a call from my mother, "Something's wrong with Aunty Dora! Can you go over and check on her" This was my mother's eighty-five-pound sister, a never-married woman who wore a big brown wig heavier than her head. It kept her from blowing away in a strong wind. Aunty Dora got mugged regularly. She used to take the bus to her bank every day to check her account balance and get a free cup of coffee, as well as steal packets of sugar. When she came to our house for dinner, she brought us a bottle of cooking Sherry. I thanked her profusely.

Lou and I rushed over to Aunty Dora's apartment

to see if she was okay. Her apartment smelled as if someone had just sprayed a new air freshener called "L'eau de Dead Body". Maybe Aunty Dora was a serial killer and had stuffed dead bodies in her closet? I checked the closets and there were no dead bodies, so that was good news. She was just sitting on her filthy couch like an Elf on a Shelf. The toilet was broken and filled with urine and feces and there was no electricity or water. There were old yellow papers thrown all over the apartment and old unpaid bills jammed in the oven, refrigerator, and dishwasher. Her bank and brokerage statements were stuffed in the couch and chairs. The refrigerator was full of mold. It was a hellhole. I had no idea this had been happening. I knew we had to get her out of there. After I puked on all the dirty dishes on the counters, I got on the phone and called around to different assisted living homes and found one in Santa Monica that would take her. The first thing Lou and I did was drive her right over there to get her cleaned up and to safety. In the car, she was really upset and kept saying "What are the other kids in school going to say when I'm not in school tomorrow?" over and over again.

"Don't worry, Aunty Dora, we'll call your school and let them know where you are," I shined her on.

"Where are you taking me?" she asked.

"You're going to a beautiful hotel in Santa Monica. You'll love it there," I told her.

We got her all set up at her new assisted living home and drove back to the apartment from hell to figure out how to deal with this disaster. It needed bulldozing. We put on gloves and masks and threw every paper we found in every appliance and piece of furniture in her apartment into a big box to deal with later. By the time we got home, there was a phone call from Aunty Dora's new assisted living home.

"Come pick up your Aunty Dora right now!" some woman screamed to me. *What next?*

Apparently, Aunty Dora decided she didn't like this woman with a walker. "You don't need that thing!" Aunty Dora screamed at the woman as she pulled her walker out from under her. The woman fell down and cracked her head open. We felt terrible.

What were we going to do with Aunty Dora, the old age home assailant? It was like "Where's Poppa?" or "Weekend with Bernie." We got her into another nursing home, got her settled, and snuck out the door before Aunty Dora tried to kill someone. The next order of business was to get a conservatorship and Durable Power of Attorney, but we needed a psychiatrist to diagnose her before we took her in front of a judge. We take her to this psychiatrist with a beard down to his belly button, and hair growing out of his ears and nose. He smelled mildewy, kind of like pachouli oil. What did we care, we just needed him to diagnose her so we could make the court date. He takes Aunty Dora into his private office. Ten minutes later he walks out with her.

"So, what do we think is wrong with her?" I asked the psychiatrist.

"I'll tell you what's wrong with her. She's f--king crazy."

It seemed like the right diagnosis.

We take Aunty Dora for the conservatorship hearing so the judge could see for himself that she was unable to handle her own affairs. (Not that she was having any affairs.) Aunty Dora fell sound asleep during the hearing and started snoring. We finally found a permanent nursing home for Aunty Dora and took her over there.

"Where the f**k am I?" she asked.

"You're at the Ritz Carlton," I lied. *Okay, I know. You should never lie. But this was a necessity.*

"Do they have room service?" she asked happily.

"No, they don't do that anymore," I lied again.

"Oh," she sighed in acceptance as she spotted a woman with a walker.

Uh-oh! We ran out as fast as we could.

Now, all we had to do was find a way to have her hellhole apartment emptied and fumigated and then put on more gloves and go through all the papers in the big box we took out of there and home with us. Life goes on and I visited Aunty Dora once a week. She was happy and they were taking good care of her at the "Ritz Carlton".

The Onions: Your Siblings. I saw a beautiful segment on TV about two sisters who were so close to each other that they gave each other diamond rings to wear signifying their wonderful friendship. I had always wished for a close sister, but mine, three years older than me, hated me from the moment I was born. I didn't even have a personality to hate yet. She would always hit and scream at me when I was a toddler, then knock me down on the floor and start beating me up for fun. *Fun for her, not for me.* I would cry and scream and kick and my mother would call out to me "Fight your own battles!" I learned early that I was on my own. Even my parents weren't going to protect me. This became my obsession for always trying to "feel safe." You may feel like this too. Feeling safe is a basic human need. If you don't feel safe, it is very hard to feel secure and happy. As we grow older, we need to find ways to make ourselves feel safe.

My sister liked to play mean tricks on me. Once she and her friend put worms in our mailbox and then told me "There's a surprise in the mailbox for you." I was only two or three, so I stuck my hand in the mailbox and got a handful of worms, slimy, disgusting little suckers. She and her friend laughed hysterically at me falling for their nasty trick. I've had this thing about hating worms all my life. I'm sure some of them are nice worms and I probably shouldn't hate them, but it's just my thing. I actually feel bad when people puncture worms with a hook and use them for fishing. I think it's animal cruelty. I'm thinking of becoming a worm activist.

Another time my mother wanted to get rid of me, so she made my sister and her girlfriend take me to the drugstore to get some candy. They left me in the drugstore alone and ran outside. Crying hysterically, I finally found them outside hiding in the alley with comic books in their hands. They told me they had stolen the comic books and that I should go into the drugstore and steal some myself. I didn't want to, but they insisted and dared me, so I walked back into the drugstore and stole a Little Lulu comic book even though I couldn't even read yet. When I walked out, they were laughing hysterically and calling me stupid. "We didn't steal the comic books, we bought them!" they laughed. I was mortified and started crying even more. When we got home, my sister told my mother that I had stolen a comic book.

"Wait 'til your father gets home!" my mother screamed at me. When my father came home, he took me upstairs, took off his belt, and started beating me with his belt again. I have always wanted a sister, just not this one.

If you have a wonderful, close family, please count your blessings. If you are like me and have, or had, a very dysfunctional family, try to make your friends into your family.

The Ketchup and Mustard: Your Career or Job. I was in interior design school and attended a lecture by Phyllis Morris, one of the top interior designers and showrooms in Los Angeles at that time. I got up my nerve and called her the next day to ask for a job. I landed it! I worked on big projects and met many of her famous clients.

I was trying to quit smoking at the time and was smoking fake cigarettes without nicotine called "Free". I had just taken them off the cashier's stand at Walgreens. *Well, they said "Free."* The smoke and smell were so bad that it permeated the whole building, and everyone walked around coughing. I had coincidentally become friends with the inventor of "Free" cigarettes, but he died of lung cancer. As you know, nothing in life is free, *except love, kindness, and laughter*.

Phyllis screamed at me too much, so I quit. I decided that I had finally taken enough abuse in my life and vowed that no one would ever treat me like that again. I was a good person, I worked hard, I was kind, maybe *too* kind, I was intelligent, and I was allowing people to disrespect me. The day I claimed my self-worth and demanded the respect I deserved; my life came alive. Miraculously, I landed an interior design project for a real estate developer who was building condominium buildings all over Los Angeles and redecorating his offices in Beverly Hills. My self-esteem was blooming. I even met my second husband. Proof that if you demand to be respected, at any age, others will respect you too. You will feel happier, more youthful, and even more successful. *No one has the right to make you feel worthless or unhappy!*

Next, a friend from design school and I decided to start the world's first custom furniture rental company. We even got a major furniture rental company to back all of our orders with unlimited funding. Our phones were ringing off the hook. There was the U.S. Military, entertainment companies, movie studios, celebrities, record companies, big businesses, staging houses for sales or parties, and some creeps.

Demanding to be treated with the respect I deserve worked. It will work for you too!

The Cardboard Box the Hamburger Came In: Your House. Going back to my life with Fart King, being disrespected, he tells me he wants to buy a house. I always went along with everything because I had been reduced to being an indentured servant. I should have been thrilled about buying a house, but deep inside I felt I was being sucked deeper and deeper into a big black hole that I wasn't going to be able to dig myself out, kind of like a grave. My *intuition* was developing.

The next thing I know, Fart King, the world's worst driver, is driving us to meet a real estate broker to look at a house. He always challenged the gas tank to see how long the car could go without running out of gas. He thought that the car never ran out of gas. We were always coasting into gas stations on fumes. Not from the gas tank, from him. He enjoyed parking on the wrong side of the street just to defy the parking signs and see how long he could go without getting a ticket. If you want to be happy and live a long youthful life, don't marry a sociopath like this.

We had an appointment to meet a real estate broker to see at a house. He made a left turn in right in front of a speeding car that was coming at us at about sixty miles an hour. As the speeding car slammed into my side of the car, I slid over and ducked my head into Fart King's lap. Don't worry, this wasn't sexual. I wasn't in the mood. I was covered with glass from head to toe, my head hurt, my neck hurt, my body hurt, I was emotionally upset. The tow truck driver took us home to get our other car. The real estate agent was waiting for us when we got there and didn't seem to notice or care about the shards of glass dropping from my hair or the cuts and bruises on my face. The house was a wreck. It looked like it had been bombed. It was sixty years old and had never been remodeled, kind of like me as I write this story.

"It's a mess. I don't like it," I said, my neck and back killing me.

We'll take it!" Fart King said, as if I was invisible and powerless.

The escrow closed and Fart King had been working on the house every day. I stopped by to see how he was doing. There was no house, just a wood frame.

"Where did our house go? I asked Fart King.

"The wrecking crew came, and they got carried away," he explained.

"Where did you find this "crew," I asked him sarcastically.

"They were standing in front of U-Haul looking for work. I didn't realize they couldn't speak English," he said sheepishly, as well he should.

I was young and had never fixed up a house, let alone re-rebuilt a very large house from scratch. I designed the entire interior with no training at all. Fart King wanted to go to Tijuana to have a wood hand-carved front door made. We met a good-looking soccer player. Alonzo who took us to a bull fight and then dipped his hands in the dead bull's blood. Fart

King invited Alonzo to stay in our house and then left me to entertain him for two weeks even though Alonzo could hardly speak English. The only thing he knew how to say was "I like cream of asparagus soup," so I took him to the market and bought him dozens of cans of Campbell cream of asparagus soup."

We would call the wood carver every week to ask him when he was going to be finished with our front door. "Soon, soon, Señor. We work on it." After about eight weeks and ready to move into the house if we had a front door, we called the wood carver and got a recording, "This phone has been disconnected." We drove to the carver's wood shop in Tijuana, and it was emptied-out.

Don, the contractor/handyman, who was building back the house by himself, went on a vacation to Catalina Island, where he dove off a pier, and was impaled by a large sharp beam. The funeral was lovely and sad, but we now lived in a house with no front door and no locks on any windows or door. Fart King's friend owned an alarm company, so he put in a free alarm system for us. The alarm was completely wired under the house and there were gangs of cats around the neighborhood that enjoyed running around under the house and tripping the wires, setting off the alarm at all hours. I never slept. You should have seen the black circles under my eyes. They could have been from melted mascara from crying, I'm not sure.

One time I heard meowing on the stairs to a tiny

basement. I opened the door and there was a cat and her ten kittens looking very scared. I fed them right away. The next morning, they were gone. My guess is they didn't like my cooking. And then there was the big earthquake shortly after we moved in and the whole house felt like it was coming apart. *It was.* The cardboard box the hamburger came in was crumbling. This was the omen, a metaphor for my life, which was crumbling.

We didn't have enough money left to furnish the house. Fart King found odd pieces of ugly furniture that were left in some old buildings in downtown L.A. that he managed. Our entry hall was an old black painted church pew. I made cute little pillows to dress it up. The pillows were kind of cute I guess but I was not meant to have a career as a seamstress. I could tell by the looks on everyone's faces when they walked into our entryway. Sometimes we just need to admit that we just aren't good at everything.

The Pickle Relish: Us. We started out a beautiful, moist, green dill pickle, but now we're so exhausted that we've become a smear of cheap pickle relish spread too thin on a burnt bun. The good news is that as we age, a lot of problems resolve, and we all have another chance to morph ourselves back into a beautiful juicy dill pickle, albeit with a few more wrinkles, fat cells, and aches and pains.

CHAPTER FIFTEEN
Living with the Frustration of Technology

OUR GROWING USE of annoying technology can put the strongest of us into a state of irritation at any age. In order to put up with the frustration of life in this quickly changing world is to either find humor in it or go live in Bangladesh.

When I was growing up, telephones actually had dials and coiled cords that got all tangled up. To people fifty and over, technology is still using a dial up phone with a party line. Generation X, Y, Z, and Alpha think a party line is snorting cocaine at a warehouse party.

I am still trying to figure out how they get a sound from miles away into a little cell phone receiver. The speed of sound is 767 miles per hour. The furthest place from Los Angeles, which is Saint-Philippe, is 30,578 miles away. It would take 40 hours for the sound to get from Los Angeles to Saint-Philippe. So, how can you talk to someone over 30,000 miles away instantly? Now, smartphones have become like organs of our bodies, like our liver or heart. We will die if we don't have one. Maybe one day they will implant smartphones into our bodies and then change the implant every year when a new model comes out.

My parents bought their first television in the late fifties, it was a status symbol, like a Tesla or a Chanel bag. We were even thrilled when electric car windows came out, especially since air-conditioned cars weren't invented yet. Once a week our TV would break and we would have to call a TV repairman and he would lean into the television set to fix it, his pants creeping down his butt, exposing the big slit in between his fat buttocks. I considered it a TV Special Event.

When the TV wasn't broken, our whole family would sit next to the stairs in the hallway and watch Sid Caesar and Abbott and Costello on a tiny TV inside this big ugly brown wood box. We enjoyed the singing and dancing Texaco men in their white suits filling up gas tanks and cleaning windshields for all of their customers. Those were the days when companies catered to us, made our lives easier, and the customer was always right. Nowadays, the customer is always wrong and treated like a criminal until they can produce and ID-ME verification and pass a facial recognition scan. I was thinking of having another facelift, but I decided against it because I wouldn't be able to use my smartphone facial recognition as a password anymore.

Did you ever watch a younger person text with their thumbs? Their fingers are tapping away as if they're transmitting Morse code, fast, like they talk. It's like they have a hurry-call and want to get the text out before they poop in their pants. As we get older, our brains don't work as fast, and our hands tend to shake a little. Typing on a smartphone is like trying to hit the target in a shooting range. It's hit or miss and the person next to us could end up dead.

Voice Activation. Now everything is voice activated. You call to make an appointment with your doctor, and you get a recording, "Please press 911 if this is an emergency," as if we don't know that.

"Press two if you're a new patient."

"Press three if you're an old patient." *Of course, I'm an old patient, I'm calling a geriatric doctor.*

"Press four if you want to talk to the billing department." *I never want to talk to them unless I overpaid.*

"Press five if you want to make an appointment."

"Press six if you know your party's extension." *What party? I love parties.*

"Press seven if you want to choose from a list of parties." *That's great, they're having lots of parties!* I press seven. I get a list of thirty people, none of them my doctor or a party, but I have to listen through the whole list to get to …

"Press eight to reach a caring team member." *Caring? Hah!*

I press eight and get another recording, "You have reached the office of Dr. Dingleberry. Your call is number fifty in line. Please wait. Your call is very important to us." *Sure, right, and the dead rat I saw lying in front of your building is important to you too.*

I'm on the phone listening to dull music that bores me to death, so I devise my own upgraded voice activation program, which is …

"Press one if you need to pee."

"Press two if you need to poop,"

"Press three if you are starving and need breakfast."

"Press four if you need to eat lunch."

"Press five if you need to eat dinner."

"Press six if you need to take your dog for a walk."

"Press seven if your dog already pooped on the floor."

"Press eight if you pooped on the floor."

"Press nine if you want to come to our office with a semi-automatic rifle."

Someone finally answers the phone, but accidentally, or purposely, disconnects it.

Artificial Intelligence (AI) is really big right now. China is even planning to beat us to the finish line, but they are too busy now building up their nuclear arsenal, which I hope (or maybe hope not) is as poorly made as all the products they ship to us. There's a company in the United States that has taught robots to dance, just what we need in this world with global warming, the risk of a nuclear war, and a declining global economy, *dancing robots*.

Now there are even electric AI cars, trucks, and vans too. I find myself looking into the windows of big trucks that we pass to make sure they have an actual driver. Why would I want to see trucks without drivers? There would be no one to shout obscenities out the window and whistle at me. I really don't trust any vehicle with a robot driving it, let alone riding in an electric Uber or Lyft car. The crashes have proven I'm 99.99% right. (I always like to say I'm 99.99% right just in case I'm wrong.) I'm all for clean energy and stopping global warming and I do worry about future generations, but I'm not ready for self-driving electric cars yet. First of all, there are not enough charging stations yet and you could get stuck somewhere in the middle of Death Valley if you can't find a charging station. Even if you can find a charging station it doesn't work, or doesn't work with your model of car, or it takes six hours to charge. What do you do, sleep in your car, or eat hot dogs at some 7/11 in the middle of nowhere for six hours waiting for your car to charge? Have a deep conversation with your AI robot? Will robots have deep thoughts and emotions? Will they be capable of love?

Electric AI cars are great for taking long driving trips. Just set your car computer for a nice relaxing eight-hour road trip and sleep in the back seat. Don't worry, you won't need an alarm clock. You'll get woken up when your car is hit head-on by a big five-hundred-ton driverless truck.

Now there are *bots* for everything. I never knew what *bots* were until recently. I thought they were little flying insects. Go to most websites and you'll see a "Chat Now" link. When you press it, a little screen pops up and asks politely "What would like to do?" *I want to get my f--king question answered!*

I needed to talk to our cable company about the extra charges on our bill they made up, so I go on chat and type out a whole explanation of what department I want, and a screen comes up that asks you which question applies to your problem. Of course, none of them do, so you say "Agent". The bot types back, "Please wait while we find a live agent." Apparently, there was a mass shooting at our cable company and the bot had to look through the dead bodies to find an agent that was still breathing. Actually, I do like the idea of AI robots sometimes. I'd really like to have one that cleans our house. At least a robot doesn't steal. *I don't think so. Maybe they do.* Is there a prison for bad robots? What if they get a life sentence? Do they rust in prison? Do they get a funeral service in a scrap metal yard?

Robots might be okay instead of a husband who does the dishes, takes out the garbage, and fixes things around the house. At least you don't need to make dinner for them every night. I don't know if they can put a penis or vagina on a robot. Female robots will probably get electrocuted when you stick an electric penis in her vagina. Electric penises will get all cut up from a tin vagina. Two robots having sex could create so much friction that both robots will explode. Maybe that's a robot orgasm. *Does a penis really need AI Intelligence? They've been operating for centuries and have never used their brains.*

One company in Las Vegas has recently found a solution to this problem. They are manufacturing custom-made human robots made out of a synthetic material that looks and feels like human skin. They are great if you don't mind the blah look on their faces. You can dress them up and put makeup on them. They have usable and washable genitals.

"Honey, what is that thing in the dishwasher?"
"Oh, that's just a vagina."

You can even buy attachments for different "experiences." Beware, if your penis gets stuck in one of them, you'll have to drive yourself to the ER naked with a rubber dummy sitting on your lap. I know someone who couldn't afford one of these dummies, so he used a vacuum cleaner hose instead. He couldn't figure out how to turn off the vacuum cleaner and ended up with a penis that looked like a broom handle. AI could also be the term for artificial insemination by a robot. Will robots have AI sperm and AI ovaries? Will they be able to make baby robots? How do you get a diaper on a robot? Or a onesie? What happens if a new, improved model of a robot comes out? Do they melt down the old ones and make tin foil out of them?

Life gets more and more complicated as we start aging, and our brains start going on overload followed by episodes of brain fog. Try teaching some older people how to use a smartphone for the first time. One time I brought home a new iPhone for Lou. He had a dumbphone that flipped up that is now worth a lot of money, but he dropped it in the toilet, so I bought him a new smartphone. He looks at it as if it's a Martian in a little box.

I unwrap the box for him. "Look, sweetie, isn't it cool?" I told him.

"What is it?"

"A new smartphone," I explain as I hand it to him.

"How do I dial it?"

"The same way you used to you flip up your cell phone, you just tap the numbers on the little buttons."

I showed him how to call his friend, also named Lou, Lou Finkelstein. It rings and I hand him the phone. Unfortunately, his friend Lou on the other end doesn't know how to answer his smartphone yet either.

"Hello, hello, HELLO! HELLO!!" I hear the other Lou screaming into *his* smartphone.

Then I hear him screaming to his wife, "Frieda, how do I answer this damn thing?!" She didn't know either. The phone disconnects. They had accidentally hung up the phone.

I called back Lou Finkelstein. "Lou, it's Rima, Lou's wife. He wants to talk to you on his new smartphone.

"You're not my wife. Her name is Frieda!" and then I hear them screaming at each other again."

Apparently, he didn't have his hearing aids on, and Frieda thought he was having an affair. She didn't have her hearing aids in either. I think they got divorced over it.

"Let's try calling someone else honey, how about your other friend, Dick?"

"Don't call me a Dick!" he screams at me. He refuses to wear his hearing aids.

"Just press the keys on the phone!'" I grit my teeth. I could actually hear my hair falling out of my head onto the floor. My hair follicles are heavy. Too much hairspray.

"Where did I put my keys?" he asks me.

"No, the keys are the little buttons on the keyboard!" I scream, losing patience.

"Where's the keyboard?"

I show him the keyboard one more time and he taps in the number.

"Tap the green button now," I explain.

He taps it. It rings. "Where do I speak into?"

It was a logical question. Does anyone know where the microphone is on a smartphone? About this time, I go to the refrigerator and get myself a glass of prune juice because this conversation has constipated me even more. Everything stresses you out more as you age. I came back into the room and the phone had fallen in his crotch and he was sleeping. You fall asleep a lot as you get older, probably because you bore yourself.

And then there are texts, mostly from scammers trying to screw you out of money or news alerts that don't matter, like there's a heat wave in some country on an island off of Africa. I keep on getting calls from a guy named "Scam Likely". Maybe he's stalking me. Actually, at my age, it makes me feel more attractive to have a stalker. Excuse me, there's a news flash …I was just interrupted by a text that said, "A billion snow crabs are missing in Alaska." Where did hell did they go? Were they kidnapped by some extremist group? Maybe it was political, and they decided not to vote for the world's dumbest candidate? Maybe they're sitting in some bomb shelter somewhere in Europe. Maybe they committed mass suicide over the world condition. Actually, I'm a little worried. I was planning to go to our favorite snow crab dinner. Speaking of crabs, is that still a venereal disease or did those crabs become extinct with the dodo bird?

Life is so hard now compared to what it used to be. I feel like I'm on a TV program, Aging Survivor. Some of the events would be Getting Out of a Low Car, Changing a Light Bulb in a High Ceiling, and Finding Your Keys and Reading Glasses.

When I was growing up, if we needed a loaf of bread, we got to choose from Wonder Bread, Wonder Bread, Wonder Bread, or no bread. Now there must be a thousand different types and brands of bread to choose from when all we want is a f--king loaf of bread. We don't want to stand there reading a bunch of ingredients, most of them chemicals that will give us a migraine at the very least, cancer at the most. There is even bread that is coated with seeds that get stuck in our crowns and implants. The ingredients all say natural flavors, but natural flavors could be anything. Sweat could be a natural flavor.

Speaking of checking out, now they have self-service checkout machines in grocery and drug stores. There's Apple Pay and all you do is point your credit card at a little machine and it takes all your money. There are no employees around anymore. If your credit card gets sucked into an ATM machine, there's no one to help. Everything is done by a machine or a robot. There's even a robot vacuum cleaner that vacuums your house for you. Don't ask me how a little round vacuum cleaner can fit into square corners. Then there's a lighted helmet that can grow your hair. Don't people grow their own hair anymore?

Younger people won't work because they can make more money trading cryptocurrencies. "Hey, I just bought two of those new crypto tokens called *Fuku* and they doubled in value, so now I have four *Fuku*. I don't know what I can do with the tokens because they're made of air, it's not the kind I can even breathe, and I can't buy anything with it other than buy more tokens of air, but I'm really going to be rich."

Young people refuse to work because they are too busy figuring out how to rob banks on the Internet, use ransomware, try to shut down our electrical grid, or bring down our whole financial system. What's the big deal? They're young, they're having fun. It doesn't matter if our entire retirement funds have vanished into some nineteen-year old's bitcoin account in some third world country. I can always sleep on that bench on a park bench if I don't mind the graffiti and the alcoholic on the next bench over.

Gen XYZs and Alphas are on the dark web having a good time buying opioids from some guy on the toilet in China, putting together homemade assault rifles, or joining a group that's planning to take over our country. What's the big deal? They're just having fun while they're waiting to overdose on Fentanyl.

Females want to be males and males want to be females and some people haven't even figured out what sex they are. Why don't we just have a baby exchange program? Your male kid doesn't like being a boy, and the little girl across the street doesn't being a girl. You just switch kids, and everybody is happy.

Now there's the *Metaverse* where many young narcissists spend their days in their parents' basements creating avatars of themselves and using their parents credit cards to buy make believe clothes and food and going places that don't even exist with their make-believe selves. They use Tik Tok or YouTube to become famous Influencers and make millions while we all worry about the price of eggs. This is what young people who don't want to work are doing now. And what are their parents doing? God knows. Probably getting stoned. Who wants to deal with it all.

Enough of this technological tirade. I feel like I'm living in a sci-fi movie, you probably do too. I'm tired of worrying about getting arrested for driving a gas car, taking someone to get an abortion, or reading a banned book. To be young and happy forever requires that we *live and let live*. Let's laugh at life and enjoy living as much as we can. Socialize, exercise, and do what we enjoy. If global warming doesn't kill us, an asteroid, or a new strain of virus, or nuclear bomb will. Why set ourselves up to regret not having enjoyed life while we still could.

Boredom, worry, and stress will destroy us if we don't decide to enjoy our lives no matter what the media outlets tell us is going to happen. Scaring viewers is what sells on TV and Internet and brings advertisers and money. Don't let the media scare you into worrying about everything that is going to happen. Let's accept the outcomes we cannot change and enjoy the rest of our lives on Planet Earth in spite of the gravity making our boobs and testicles fall. We now know we can go back billions of light years, but it's only a matter of time before we will be able to go forward billions of years. I suspect we will not like what we would see. So, let's age happily, youthfully, and healthily. *F--k technology. F--k aging. Enjoy life now. There are no "do overs".*

CHAPTER SIXTEEN
Exhale. Let's Have Fun Again!

W E CAN STILL have fun like we used to have when we were younger. There a no law against fun (depending on what kind of fun you want to have). God never ages, so if we're made in his image, we never age either—*don't you wish*. He made our planet beautiful and bountiful so we could be happy forever. When we disrespect our earth's beauty, he shows his wrath with hurricanes, tornados, and floods. When we allow evil to win over good, he threatens us with droughts and earthquakes. When we have anger and hate in our hearts and kill other living beings, he sends us a pandemic as a reminder that the life he gave us can go extinct, like the dinosaurs. Please God, let good win over evil. We good people just want to enjoy life and our blessings, have fun, and feel young and happy. We will be kind and loving, help others, and take care of the planet you created for us, and have fun as long as our bodies last.

Young Fun. Max was a "spare" husband to me when nineteen and married to Fart King. Once a year we had The Annual Dirty Underwear Return Outing. He put all his used dirty underwear in a bag, and we took it to Macy's to return. "This underwear is no good!" he would scream and argue with the sales-woman. She would give up and call the manager, who was so intimidated by Max that he refunded the money for the dirty underwear he returned other than the ones that he threw out the window on the way over. "You don't ask, you don't get," he would laugh on the way home. (I'm sorry Macy's, we were kids having fun.)

Another time the three of us were at the Charthouse at the Marina. While waiting for a table we sat in front of the bathrooms, watching men and women go in and out of the restrooms. It was like Grand Central Station. Just for fun, when no one was looking, we switched the Men and Women signs so that they were all going in and out of the wrong bathrooms. Not very nice, but it was so much fun watching the confused looks on everyone's faces as they walked in and out. (I'm sorry Charthouse too, we were kids having fun.)

It was the sixties, and the hippies were all over Sunset Boulevard, hanging out and smoking grass (I tried smoking grass, but the blades of our lawn got stuck in my teeth) and jumping in and out of cars, having sex, hitchhiking, whatever. Everyone hitchhiked in those days. Gloria, Max's new wife, and I were in the back seat taking in the whole scene when Fart King picked up a hitchhiker and shoved him into the backseat with us just to be funny. Gloria and I looked over and the hitchhiker was covered in blood and it was dripping all over us and the car.

"I've been slashed by a queen in drag" he slurred.

I didn't know what a Queen in drag was, so I thought maybe the Queen of England stabbed him. We took him to the hospital and that was the end of our picking up hitchhikers' days, *except* for the time…

Fart King and I were driving home from Haight Asbury in San Francisco. He picked up a guy hitch-hiking on the highway. The weirdo climbed in the backseat and waved his big sharp machete at us proudly. We told him how nice it was and humored him for many miles until we found a restaurant and then asked him if he'd like to have dinner with us, our treat. When he got up to go to the bathroom, we ran out of there, hopped in the car, and sped off as fast as we could, burning rubber all the way. A suggestion, if you want to age well and live long with as few scars as possible, don't pick up hitchhikers.

Back to Lou, my second husband. Our honeymoon was wonderful. We went for a two-week ski trip to an upscale ski lodge in Utah where we met this great couple from New York. We had so much fun together. One night we had so much wine that she climbed on a luggage cart, and I wheeled her down an elevator and into the kitchen of the hotel kitchen.

The kitchen staff didn't laugh, and the chef waved his butcher knife in the air at us. Why can't all of us aging people still have fun times like that? I know firsthand that life can be very hard, but do we have to be so serious all the time?

Another night we were having dinner at this elegant restaurant with this couple and a few other people. After dinner the busboy hadn't cleared the dishes off yet. I had consumed a lot of wine, so I decided to show everyone how I could pull the tablecloth off the table without moving any dishes or glasses. Some guy I had gone out with once had shown me how to do it, but that was only with two glasses on a paper place mat, but I was determined to entertain everybody. I stood up and took hold of the tablecloth and amazingly pulled it out as quickly as I could from under all the glasses and plates which were still sitting on the bare table unmoved. Everyone was amazed, including me. I think we got kicked out of the restaurant. I wouldn't try this trick again if my life depended on it. (Well, maybe, maybe if a group of terrorists hijacked a plane I was on, and they threatened to blow it up the plane if I didn't to my tablecloth trick.)

Older Fun. Those fun, light-hearted years are gone and as we age, we become much more complex and serious. It doesn't have to be that way. Humor and happiness can be ours if we change our attitude on aging and find a way to laugh at ourselves and life and have fun every day no matter how old we are and how much our bodies ache and how many diseases we've survived. If we start smiling instead of frowning, our wrinkles will look softer, and we'll look and feel younger and lighter. A good face cream helps too.

Let's experience new adventures and refuse to give in to aging and being old and unhappy. When I was younger, I was up for *almost* any new adventure and I felt alive, young, and happy. I had great stories to tell.

Divorced Fun. In between marriages, I met this guy that told me he was into swinging. Last time I went swinging was at the park with my parents. He explained to me what it was. I wasn't exactly sexually liberated, actually I was a prude, and besides, I guessed you had to bring a partner to swing with. I asked him to take me to a swing party just to see what it was and told him I would never participate. I was just curious about how these things work.

So, Swinger Sam took me to this swing party up in the Hollywood Hills. Everyone was walking around naked. I pretended not to notice. The guys with their little elephant trunks swinging and the girls with their boobs bouncing were all talking to each other as if they didn't notice they weren't naked. Guys would come up to me and ask me why I wasn't taking my clothes off and asked if I wanted to have sex with them. Swinger Sam takes me to peak into "the community room". I thought I would see people having a neighborhood meeting, but it was a jungle of nude, tangled up people.

Some other guy asked me "Would you like to go in?"

"No thank you," I said politely. I'm just observing," I told him as if I was monitoring at class at Harvard.

Swinging Sam also used to also go to a nudist camp in Topanga Canyon. I had never been to a nudist camp, so I asked him to take me there too. The lawn was filled with out of shape naked people lying on the grass around an algae-filled dirty swimming pool. I was the only one there in clothing and again the guys would come up and try to talk me into taking off my clothes.

"No, I'm just observing" I would say politely.

A naked grandfather, his hanging balls swinging like a pendulum, proudly showed me photos of his grandchildren. I watched the nude people playing volleyball, their loose parts bouncing around as they ran for the ball and jumped to slam it across the net. *I decided that most people look better with clothes on and that was that.*

I crave fun, adventure, new people, and new experiences again. I like my people with clothes on though. You probably do too as you age.

My friend Camper Cathy decided we should go on a camping trip together with my daughter and her two little boys for two weeks. I hate camping. You can't call room service or make restaurant reservations. She drives up to my house with this huge Winnebago.

I shrugged and we loaded up the supplies, all our

kids, and my frazzled nerves, and we headed up to the Russian River, wherever the hell that was. *Maybe we were going to drive to Russia. I wouldn't mind seeing the Kremlin.* I had never been on a camping trip other than in a tent a long time ago and I hated it, I wanted my toilet and my shower and my makeup. I had never been in an RV, and never even wanted to be in an RV, but I guess I was a follower, so what the hell, it was a new experience.

She drove, I cleaned and cooked, it was a perfect relationship had we been lesbians, but we weren't, well at least *I* wasn't. The kids all screamed and yelled and hit each other the entire drive. I was in charge of shutting them up but wasn't very good at it. I was good at cleaning the RV and cleaning up her boy's messes and she was good at driving, fishing, and cooking hot dogs on an open fire and, oh, emptying out the sewage tank.

One night she had forgotten to make reservations at the campgrounds, so we had to pull over in some unmarked field to sleep. It was just us two women, just like Thelma and Louise, but with kids. We were awakened at 6:00 am by a loud banging on the Winnebago door. We open the door, half asleep, and there are four hairy mean-looking men with shot guns aimed at us and the kids.

"Y'all betta get outta here right quick! This here's private property! Y'all got five minutes, or we shoot!"

I guessed I didn't have time to brush my teeth and put on my makeup. We burned rubber all the way out of the field, our hearts pounding, our kids crying and screaming. We drove a little further north and found this little hippy town. All I knew was that there was civilization and a cowboy dance club. I was in heaven. I couldn't disembark the Winnebago fast enough to see humans that weren't threatening to kill us.

We left the kids in the RV parked right in front of the dance place and took turns checking on the kids every ten minutes. It wasn't long until I was dancing with this hippy cowboy, and he invited us to his house for a party. We followed him down this long narrow dark dirt road and parked the RV in front of this big cabin with old vans parked all over the dirt. For all we knew they were the Manson cult. Luckily, everyone was too stoned to notice we were alive, so we survived and started back home. *Camping hadn't been on my bucket list.*

Getting Too Old Fun. It's hard to recreate these crazy times as we age. Older people are supposed to be serious all the time. We are supposed to be wise and learned, the mentors and teachers of younger generations. It's time to stop wallowing in self-pity and focusing on our every ache and pain. Socializing and laughing with others is the greatest pain reliever. Going to a funny movie or having a great dinner out with good friends is healing. If you have enough money to travel and your health is good, make a bucket list of countries and cities you want to see before you kick-the-bucket. *("Aha!" That's why it's called a "bucket list"!)* Going to new places, meeting new people, and enjoying new foods will cure your humdrum life and take you away from your worries. *Just do it if you can!*

CHAPTER SEVENTEEN
Managing Your Memories, Good and Bad

D
O YOU KNOW where I put my memory? Why did I walk in this room? Oh, that's right, I walked in here to work on writing my book. For a minute I couldn't remember. Now where'd I put my eyeglasses? Oops, they're on my head, next to my keys. I knew my head felt a little heavy.

We all have memories (unless we have amnesia). Some may be wonderful, some humorous, and some may be sad, even terrible, and still haunt our lives. So how do we get rid of the bad memories and enjoy the good ones? I've devised a way to erase the memories that destroy our happiness so we can enjoy only our good memories, it's called *Grouch Busters*. This system will help us get over our bad memories and give us the strength to let them go. It can help us find more joy and fulfilling friendships no matter how old we are. Let's organize our memories and file them where they need to be.

Our Bad Memory Box

Start with using a brown paper bag. You can use greasy bags from the donut store, or one of the bags we use to cover our heads when we're having a bad hair day, anything we have that will help us sort through and organize all of our bad thoughts and memories. These are rejections, losses, hurtful and painful moments, lonely times, failures, despair, embarrassing times – it's all part of the process of living and aging, I call it *Agingitis.*

The first step is to write down each of your *bad memories* on a separate piece of paper. Then put the pieces of paper in your Bad Memory Bag. Put it up in the attic, or down in the basement, or even flush it down the toilet (use biodegradable paper please), give it to your dog to eat, or burn the damn bag. These bad memories are useless to you now. You don't need them haunting your brain or your soul anymore. Here are a few of the bad memories that have haunted me for years. These are the kind of things that I promise to throw away with my Bad Memory Bag, after I've told you about them, of course.

Childhood Horrors. I was about seven years old in Chicago and it was Halloween. My Brownie Troop was having a Halloween party. After the party, one of the Brownie mothers was driving me and some of the other girls home. It was pouring rain outside and very dark. The mother pulled up across the street from the apartment building that two of the Brownies lived in and left the engine running. This was a heavily traveled street, and she stupidly let the two Brownies out of her car to cross the street alone. I was only seven years old, what did I know? All of a sudden, a rush of traffic came speeding by as the two girls were in the middle of the street. I remember all of us Brownies in the car screaming and yelling as we saw both of our friends get hit by multiple cars and sliding hundreds of feet down the street like two limp rag dolls. They both were killed while I was sitting in the car with the other girls, all watching in horror. It hurts as I write this and to this day I never want to go out on Halloween, especially if it is raining. There is no way to find humor in this. I've put this in my Bad Memory Bag. I'm tired of crying about it. Its history and *history can never be changed.*

To look at our lives in hindsight is useless, we can't erase the things that have happened to us or to others we love, we can't change everything we did wrong. In order to laugh our way through life as we age, we need to free ourselves of pain and guilt, force ourselves to look forward to a good life as we age, and not look back on our bad memories and mistakes. Everyday becomes more and more precious as our lives go by faster and faster. We need to do the things that make us happy, not what other people think will make us happy. *Laugh more and you will age less.*

I slept over at my friend Diana's house one night. The building next door caught fire. We ran outside to watch the firemen saving people. They pulled out a burnt man on a gurney as I watched. It was a horrible sight. It has stayed with me forever and I am overly cautious about fires. I stuffed this in the Bad Memory Bag too. It's too ugly to remember.

Mistakes. Most of us can remember all the good opportunities we had that we didn't make happen. Our memories usually start with "What if …? What if we finished college? What if we married that person? What if we didn't marry that person? What if we didn't lie about …? What if we didn't steal …? File all your "What if" thoughts away. Regrets will only lead you to unhappiness as you age. Write them down, tear them up, throw them in The Bad Memory Bag, and toss them in the garbage. Every day is a new opportunity no matter how old you are. There is no going back to the past.

The choices we make when we are younger are not necessarily the choices we would make now. As we grow older there are fewer choices, but that doesn't mean there are no choices. No matter what age or sex orientation you are, staying in an abusive relation is contrary to the goal of aging happily. If you are being abused mentally or physically, or both, at any age, it's time to rethink the life you still have left. The goal is not to just survive, but to enjoy life. Remember what our Spiritual Leader told us, "No one, not even your family or your children, have the right to make your life unhappy."

It is important that we be with people that make us feel good about ourselves and treat us with the kindness and respect that we deserve as human beings. Anything else is unacceptable. If you are not in a relationship of any kind and are feeling lonely, remember that is better to feel lonely when you are alone than to be with someone who makes you feel bad about yourself and treats you with disrespect.

Regrets. It was the day of my first wedding. I was nineteen years old, and I had never been to a wedding. I wore a white silk suit that was two sizes too big for me and matching cheap silk shoes that hurt my feet. When our Spiritual Leader said to repeat after him "duly consecrated" I said, "duly concentrated." At the reception, my mother leaned over and whispered in my ear, "I really don't like this guy. I don't trust him." Her timing was priceless.

When my new husband, who you know by now as Fart King, and I got home to our new apartment he ripped off his clothes, jumped on the bed, and let out the loudest, smelliest fart I've ever heard or smelled. The honeymoon was over, and he wanted sex after The Big Fart.

"I'm dead tired," I said, obviously turned off.

"I've been dead since I married you," complained Fart King.

"We've only been married four hours so you're still eligible for artificial resuscitation" I replied. *What was I thinking? I was only nineteen and had known him for only three months.* The next thing he did was put me on a clothing allowance like I was a child (even though I worked), so I put him on a sex allowance like he was a sex-addict (which he wasn't).

This guy was obsessed with farts and boogers. His idea of having fun was passing a big fart with me in the car and then rolling up the windows and locking them or rolling boogers into tiny balls and leaving them on his nightstand for me to clean up, along with his dirty underwear and socks strewn on the floor. His farts and boogers were his tortures of choice. He was definitely a perfect candidate for my Bad Memory Box.

One day Fart King left his wallet open on the dresser and I happened to look over and notice a photo of a little girl about five or six with long brown hair and hazel eyes.

"Who is this?" I asked.

"Oh, that's some photo of a little girl I found in the garbage. I thought she was cute, so I keep it in my wallet" he answered. *Hmmm, he goes through other people's garbage. Did I marry a dumpster diver?*

I thought it was a little weird, but kind of understood that sometimes people lie to cover up things, so I just let it go. The photo of the little girl would linger in my mind forever because I knew there was some mystery to it. *Who puts a picture of a little girl that he found in the garbage in his wallet and keeps it forever?* I found out the secret of the photo many years later.

Physical and Mental Abuse. Another bad memory I put in my Bad Memory Bag was the day Fart King came over to pick up our daughter per our joint custody agreement. I was in the bedroom watching TV while our toddler, who was about three years old then, was taking a nap. For no reason, Fart King started calling me the "C" word over and over again.

"C--t! C--t!! C--t!!! he screamed, coming at me in a rage.

"You get out of my house right now!" (In all honesty it was still half his house I realized later.)

"C--t! C--!! C--!!!" he yelled repetitiously as if I hadn't gotten the drift yet, glaring at me with the red face and bulging eyes of a psycho ready to attack. (Fart King was a misogynist and used to tell me that "All women are C—ts", so I already knew he was a misogynist, and it wasn't personal.)

"Out, right now, or I'm calling the police" I screamed back.

"C--t! C—t!! C—t!!!" he yelled over and over again, lunging at me, throwing me down on the ground as I reached for a phone to call the police. He pulled the phone cord out of the wall and threw it across the room, it hit the wall and his hands grabbed my neck, and he squeezed harder.

I reached for our other phone, grabbed the receiver, tried to dial the police, but he pulled it out of the phone jack and threw it against the wall too, then squeezed my neck tighter and tighter. I started screaming louder and louder, gasping for air. He was *really* trying to kill me!

Suddenly, I heard crying and screaming "Daddy! Stop it! Daddy! Stop it!"

Our three-year-old daughter was running into the bedroom. Fart King released his hands. Had she not come into the room to save me he would have killed me, *I am quite sure.* What I've taken away from this story is that mean people are mean people. They don't change. They can do sweet things sometimes, even overly sweet, to keep us from finding out what they really are inside. Some are very guarded and secretive in order to keep us from knowing that they are having mean thoughts about us. Some of them are very phony and rely on money and power to control us. Some are saying they're really happy for us when underneath they are hoping we will fail. They are very unhappy and jealous people. They are toxic. Accept that some people are evil. Get them out of your life! I have put this horrific, almost-deadly event in my Bad Memory Bag.

Degrading Moments. I remember our parents used to take us to El Bianco, an Italian restaurant that was right under the noisy Chicago "El". I ordered a big plate of spaghetti smothered in tomato sauce, took two bites, and was full. I was a skinny kid and just didn't eat much.

"Your eyes are always bigger than your stomach!" my father yelled at me as he took this huge bowl of pasta covered with marinara sauce and dumped it over my head. I was mortified and cried but realized I looked kind of good in red hair when I got home. From that day forward and still today, it doesn't matter how much was on my plate, I eat everything on it or take it home in a doggy bag and *really* give it to our doggy. *She loves pasta carbonara.* I put this humiliating event in my Bad Memory Bag too.

Physical Pain. My parents would take us to

Coney Island. I wanted to go on the giant wood slide. I climbed up the stairs wearing my favorite little shorts and slid down the slide like I was sliding down from an expert ski slope in the Alps. When I got up my legs and rear end were bright red and bleeding. Someone should have warned me not to go down a wooden slide with bare legs. I really developed an aversion to amusement parks. This one goes in the Bad Memory Bag too.

Frightening Childhood Experiences. One time my parents took us to Jones Beach in New York where all these big people were laying around on their fat bodies, drinking beer, and playing volleyball. I loved it. Then I had to go pee, so my mother sent me alone to this disgusting outhouse at the back of the beach. When I walked out of the outhouse I didn't know where I was or where my family was. I was too young to know right from left or east from west. I wandered around Jones Beach crying, looking for my mommy and daddy. They didn't seem to miss me. Maybe it was their plot to get rid of me. As the sun started going down, my parents finally realized I was missing. It was finally almost dark when a nice lifeguard helped me find them. I really never liked the beach much after that and there's nothing grittier and more uncomfortable than sand in your crotch. This was a very scary event for a young child. I'm tossing it in my Bad Memory Box right now.

Emotionally Hurt. I was riding my bicycle along with my good friend, LeRoy, when we lived in Jeffrey Manor, just outside Chicago. We were both about four years old and having fun. (In hindsight, I realize that LeRoy must have been black. I didn't notice. I just knew we had fun together. I am sure that no one is born a racist. It is something some parents teach their children unfortunately. (Luckily, my parents didn't.)

We decided to ride our bicycles over the state line into Indiana and ended up in a gas station trying to get some bottles of Coca-Cola out of the vending machine. We didn't have any money to put in the Coke machine because we were too young to understand that nothing in life is free. (Other than kindness, love, and laughter.) The next thing we know is a police car pulls up next to us. *What was this about? Did they think a couple of four-year-olds were robbing the gas station?*

When I got home my father took off his belt and started hitting me with it and screaming at me about how bad I was to wander off like that. It really hurt, physically and emotionally, so I got the message that I was bad, really bad. There were many other belt beatings to come and there were never any hugs, never an "I love you" and it shaped my life. I used to scrape a fork down my thigh to show him what he did to me. (I guess I was into guilt-giving even then too.)

My parents were a different generation born in the very early twentieth century and believed in physical punishment for their children. Maybe your parents were like this too. They didn't know how to show love to their children. At least mine didn't. As we age and grow wiser, we need to realize that we can't blame our parents for everything. They did their best with what they knew how to do. It was different times. Forgive them and move forward. Let's put emotional stuff like this in our Bad Memory Box.

All of the above are the kind of memories that make us all feel unimportant, degraded, frightened, traumatized, and embarrassed. We can cry a little about them before we toss them. I threw my Bad Memory Bag in the garbage last night and waited outside early this morning so I could watch the garbage man throw it in the truck and haul off to the garbage dump. It's like cleaning out your closet and throwing out old, outdated, torn and stained clothing that you haven't worn for years. Once they're out of the house, you never remember that you had them. Now is the time for us to still make more good memories no matter how old we are. *The past is gone. Let's live in the now!*

The Good Memory Box. When life gives you ice cream, eat lots of it (unless you're lactose intolerant.) Write down each and every one of your good memories, the times you were happy and had fun, the times with good friends, the times you were able to laugh, and put them all in a Good Memory Box and keep it on your coffee table or nightstand. Make it the most beautiful box you can find. Even add some photos of people and places that you love so that you can always bring back good memories. Enjoy looking in this box whenever you feel sad and nostalgic to remind yourself of the good life you've had. Be sure to add all of your fond and funny memories to this box. These are the kind of memories of how carefree we used to be and how much fun we used to have when we were young. Put them in your good memory box, but don't lock it. Here are some of my examples.

What the Hell Was I Thinking? I was finally divorced from Fart King and free. I put on my padded bra and hot pants and went to a disco with my girlfriend. This guy started following me around, begging me to dance with him, so I finally gave in. I wasn't smart enough to give him a phony number. He called and called and bragged that his father was the one who designed the Hindenburg, the blimp that exploded into flames in 1937 and killed 35 people on its maiden flight. My intuition tried to tell me that luck and brains didn't run in his family. *Unfortunately, I didn't follow my intuition. Big Mistake.*

Two weeks later he had moved himself into my house, removed my beloved mattress (the one that promised me it would never talk) and replaced it with a waterbed even though I get seasick and throw up even if I put one foot on a ferry. It was like sleeping on the Titanic. He parked his old beat-up VW van filled with all these rusty tools and God-knows-what in my upscale neighborhood driveway.

He was a Recycler addict, a local newspaper that everyone bought and sold things on before the Internet, kind of like a pre-Internet Craig's List. Every morning he would go out and bring me back used things that I didn't want, kind of like a pet cat bringing home dead rats to please you. One day he brought home a huge hamster Habitrail for my daughter, complete with about ten hamsters spinning on wheels. There is nothing I wanted more than a dining room table filled with rodents. My daughter glanced at it once and said "*Eww*". My cats, Samantha and Munchkin, couldn't wait to eat them. *I secretly hoped that they would eat Hamster Guy too.* I don't know how this guy ended up in my house, it just happened. He was kind of like a bad case of herpes.

I was stupid enough to bring Hamster Guy with me to meet a bunch of my friends at a hotel in Palm Desert. As we pulled up to the valet park in front of the hotel in his beat-up old junkyard van all the valet park guys were laughing their ass off, and they were young, so they still had cute asses. I slunk down in the seat as low as I could so that no one would see me. Things got more embarrassing from there.

The next morning, we all meet out at the pool and the cabana boys give us all our beach chairs and towels and we order fancy drinks with umbrellas and maraschino cherries. Hamster Guy struts out to the pool as if he's John Travolta in "Saturday Night Fever" with his new-used Recycler ghetto blaster blaring, "Stayin' Alive". I was singing "Wishin' I was Dead" in my head as I pretended I didn't know this A-hole. Then things got worse.

My friends all decided they wanted to go out to dinner at a really nice restaurant that night, but none of them had cars big enough to fit everyone. Hamster Guy insisted he take everyone in his VW "luxury van". None of them had seen his van yet and I knew they would never want to see it again. We all met at the front door of the hotel, all dressed up, and Hamster Guy, wearing a bright polyester print disco shirt, jumps out and struggles to pull open the sliding door (which I think was attached to the van with masking tape) and holds out his hand to help us all in, or maybe it was to keep the door from completely falling off, I'm not sure. They all look at each other, start laughing, and climb into the van. You should have been there to see the looks on their faces when they saw all the rusty old tools and old worn-out old clutter in the van. We still laugh about it now. It gets worse from here.

Hamster Guy and I made it home safely to Los Angeles. I prayed all the way home, so that helped a little. I was very dirty from all the grease, covered with sweat and sand, my rear-end hurt a lot from the worn-out shock absorbers. My frizzy hair (which had looked so nice and straight in the dry desert air) looked like a tumbleweed. It had been 100 degrees out in the desert and his air conditioning consisted of rolling down all his windows.

When we got back to my house, which he now *thought* was his house, he tells me, "I have a big surprise for you."

I'd had enough surprises for a lifetime, no, two lifetimes, but I humored him. "What now?" I yawned.

"We're going to Europe next week!"

"We are?" I said instead of saying what I wanted to say, which was "Over my dead body." I didn't say this because I really didn't know him well enough to be sure he wasn't a serial killer. I didn't want to give him any suggestions.

"Yes, for two weeks. I'm going to buy a lot of old Mini-Coopers to sell in the United States. You'll help me drive them to the port in London."

I'd never been to Europe, so I decided to go with the plan and have a new life experience. I didn't know when I'd have another opportunity to go to Europe if my divorcee life was going as bad as it was. It could be all downhill from here, but it didn't have far to go.

I packed up my clothes, left my daughter, the cats, and the hamsters with Fart King, got on the plane, and settled in the seat, the plane took off, and I was actually excited about seeing London, Paris, and Amsterdam. Then the real surprise comes.

"I forgot to tell you something," he said, as I was looking out the window at Los Angeles 20,000 feet below us.

"What now?" I replied, fearful of what he was going to tell me next.

"The tickets are stolen," he confessed.

"What!" I screamed, about to jump out of the plane in order to avoid being arrested, but remembered I got nauseous even on the parachute jump at Coney Island, and anyway, I didn't want to mess up my hair.

"Don't worry about it, it's cool," he assures me.

So now I'm a criminal. I put it out of my mind and tried to enjoy the experience before they threw me into prison. I was afraid Scotland Yard would pick us up in London the minute we got off the plane. (Why is Scotland Yard in London? Shouldn't it be in Scotland?)

We checked into a kind of decent hotel in London and things are okay—*for now*. He took me to restaurants and shows and we went to see the sights. *So far, so good.* It would have been much more fun if he had taken a shower and brushed his teeth at least a few times on the trip. The days were filled with buying old rusty Mini-Coopers and following behind Hamster Guy to the Port of London in one of the cars. There were just a few problems.

We were at the tip of Scotland (don't ask me how we ended up there) and I'm following his tiny red Mini Cooper in my tiny red Mini Cooper around a round-a-bout and all of a sudden there's about ten more tiny red Mini Coopers speeding around the round-a-bout as if it was the Tour de France, exiting the round-a-bout in four different directions. I had to make a quick decision which one to follow because they all look exactly alike. I had a 25% chance of being right.

As I sat on the side of a road at the tip of Scotland, no currency to use, no phone, no idea where I was, Hamster Guy was gone, and I was lost. I did what any woman would do, cried. And then I remembered that every cloud has silver lining; I had gotten rid of Hamster Guy.

After about an hour of crying I saw there was a pub down the road. I drove over there, parked the car, and went into the pub. There were lots of good-looking men in little plaid skirts to watch. I spent about an hour trying to look up their kilts to see what they were wearing under them when Hamster Guy finally found me. I probably would have been better off if he hadn't. I'd still be in Scotland happily dancing the Highland Fling.

I still needed to go to Amsterdam with him, so I humored Hamster Guy. I wanted to get home, even if it was with a stolen airplane ticket. We had to take a boat train to Amsterdam. I thought it was some kind of boat placed on a train, who knew? A boat train turned out to be a train where the game was to try to sleep while I was crushed into a tiny train compartment with six men on three cots piled on top of each other on both sides while I listened to them snore and fart all night. The next day we boarded an old boat and as I tried to sleep in the hull while huge waves hit the bottom of the boat, I was seasick and felt like puking. I prayed we didn't hit an iceberg.

After freezing my way through sightseeing in Amsterdam in December and not being able to feel my feet or hands (similar to now, but that's my neuropathy) we were going to go home the next day. Hallelujah. All I could think of was the police picking me up at the airport in L.A. and putting me in prison for flying with the stolen tickets. I hoped the handcuffs would match my outfit. We got back safely.

"It's over! Drain out your waterbed and go!" I was tired of being seasick on the f---king waterbed and dealing with dead hamsters. (I still have no idea where he hid my regular mattress. How do you hide a whole mattress?) Then I did what most divorcees do when they are a failure at selling real estate, I enrolled in an Interior Design Program at UCLA.

I put this whole experience in my Good Memory Box only because I love to remember this story and always laugh at it *in hindsight*. Anything that makes us still laugh goes into our Good Memory Box.

Why Did I Say "Yes"? Next came Carpet Guy (named for the bruises I got on my back from his living room carpet.) We dated for a while and even tried to start a company together making suede wrap around pants from a pattern we made from this pair of wrap-around cotton pants I had been wearing. What I didn't realize is that when I was wearing the pants and crossed my legs, I was giving everyone a crotch shot. One morning I pick up the phone and its Carpet Guy. "You were in a big auto accident last night!" he informed me.

"Right," I said, and the monster from The House of Wax swung into my window and attacked me too." (A recurrent dream I had since I was five years old.)

"Get dressed, you have an appointment for an x-ray today," he said.

"What's wrong with me?" I asked.

"You've got whiplash and your neck and back are killing you. You can hardly walk."

I assumed his sidekick had been in the car with us last night, but it was hard to remember since I wasn't in the car. I didn't want anything to do with this phony accident, but he insisted my name was on the police report already as a victim. I gave up and went.

Carpet Man and his sidekick, Marshmallow Butt, were walking around the X-ray lab wearing gowns that were open in the back and their rear ends sticking out like puffy marshmallows. (It reminded me of the S'mores we used to roast at sleep-away camp.) A week later he told me to go meet with their attorney in Marina Del Rey. It gets weirder.

The accident attorney was sitting behind a big desk with a view of the entire Marina behind him. He was a nice-looking older man with glasses and long sandy brown hair and seemed to be coming on to me because he was licking his lips the whole time. (Or maybe his lips were chapped, or it was a nervous habit.) He was asking me about my smoking since I was still a chain smoker. He told me he was going to take me to Schick, and he would pay for it. I didn't know I needed a shave.

At the Schick anti-smoking program, I was locked in this tiny booth and forced to smoke as many cigarettes as fast as I could in an hour. I guess this was called aversion therapy. I felt nauseated and dizzy and disoriented from all the nicotine when they finally let me out of the booth the only feeling I got was an aversion to Schick and the attorney.

The next week the lawyer called me and told me to come to his office to pick up my check. Who was I to not accept a check? Money was tight and my alimony was going to run out. I get into his office, light up a cigarette, and we start talking. He hands me the insurance check, stands up as if walking me out, then suddenly pushes me down on his office sofa, climbs on top of me, and starts humping me as if he was my dog. I fought him off, threw the check at him, and ran out. I put this into my Good Memory Box because it's another funny predicament I allowed myself to get into. It still makes me laugh.

Stupid and Impulsive. How many times have you said something stupid, or tripped and fell, or made a ridiculous mistake and then punished yourself forever, staying up nights thinking that you looked like a fool, and you probably did.

One time I was with Fart King at a holiday dinner with some friends and their family and their little girl, about two years old, was on the floor and leaned over and she was wearing the cutest little ruffled panties. She was so cute that I took my foot to give her a soft little pat, but she fell over and started crying. To this day everyone that was there thinks I'm a toddler abuser. I laugh at the memory, so I keep it.

Embarrassment. I was boy crazy when I was twelve years old, but they weren't crazy about me. Maybe it was my buck teeth and frizzy hair. My friend Barbara and I went to the beach and met two cute boys and we all went wading in the waves together, hand in hand, just like in the movies. I was wearing a bathing suit stuffed with foam rubber "falsies" as we used to call them. Suddenly a big wave hit and washed over me, I looked down and one of my falsies was gone, I could see it floating in Lake Michigan like a matzo ball floating in chicken soup. I wonder if anyone ever found it. It would be an antique now and worth a lot of money. I saw the boy look startled at my half a pair of breasts and I was mortified and started crying and ran up into the cabana and wouldn't come out until dark and everyone left. How embarrassing this was to a twelve-year-old. What I learned from this mortifying pre-teen experience is that if we want to be happy, we need to laugh at our foibles.

Awkwardness. A friend of mine was dating a plastic surgeon (it's always helpful to know one as you age) and he said he would give me a boob job for free. Anything free is okay with me unless it's a rectal exam or a sex change operation. He told me to go to a department store and try on different size bras and stuff them with socks to find out what size implants I wanted. The salesgirl thought I was either nuts or a sock thief as she watched suspiciously as I was stuffing socks into the bras I was trying on. I was worried she would call the police, but I was a woman on a mission, and nothing would stop me.

I walked into the surgeon's office the next day with a size C bra dangling from my hand. His nurse showed me to an exam room and told me to strip down to my waist and get on the table. I took everything off and, bare-chested, climbed up and tried to sit on the bottom edge of the exam table. The nurse forgot to tell me that the bottom part of the exam table was one of those that slid out like breadboard slides out from a countertop. (Maybe they made salami sandwiches in the exam room?) When the surgeon walked in, I had just fallen off the table and was lying flat on my back on the floor, bare chested. I was mortified again. He laughed (probably at my breasts).

The breast augmentation went well other my friend had told me she had been in the operating room with the surgeon, her new sort-of boyfriend, apparently it was a new kind of date, and they couldn't get one of my new boobs to stand up straight to take a photo of them, kind of like trying to hold up Jell-O parfaits on my chest. I don't know what happened to the photos. There are probably millions of men on the Internet masturbating over them. They should only know what they look like now.

When I got home, I looked in the mirror and my whole chest had turned black, and my new boobs were killing me. (I had never heard of anyone who was murdered by boobs, but maybe smothered by quadruple D implants?) My boyfriend at that time rushed me to the surgeon's office. My blood was pooling in my chest.

They wheeled me back into the operating room for an emergency surgery to put in drains and I was okay, but the surgeon now tells me that I'm supposed to spend the rest of my life lying face down on a hard floor on my boobs for an hour a day to keep them soft. I did the math, and I would have had to spend thousands or even millions of hours, depending on how long I lived, lying on a hard floor, and pressing on my boobs to keep the implants soft. This wasn't do-able, for me at least. It wasn't how I wanted to spend the rest of my life and even if I did, I didn't want to end up with a flattened nose.

Foot in Mouth Moment. There was this woman at the nail salon I used to talk to that was pregnant with triplets. I hadn't seen her there for quite a while, I don't know how long, but one day I walked in the nail salon and there she was as big as a hippopotamus in a flowered tent dress.

I smiled and asked her, "Hi, when are the triplets due?"

"I already had them," she said with darts in her eyes.

"Congratulations!" I told her. *What else could I say?* I faded into the woodwork like a termite in trouble with his girlfriend for eating too much wood.

Why Did I Blurt That Out? One time Fart King and Max and I were at a dinner party at someone's house in Beverly Hills and they were serving assorted berries with whipped cream.

"What kind of berries are those?" someone asked.

"Strawberries and blueberries," the host replied.

"And dingleberries!" I blurted out. God knows where from inside me that came from. I didn't even know what a dingleberry was. I had just heard Fart King and Max making jokes about dingleberries. I really thought they were a type of berry. I saw the faces of all twelve people at the dinner table drop and they were all snarling at me. I was mortified. I felt like climbing under the table, but their two dogs were under there growling at me too. I still laugh at this.

How Could I Have Been So Stupid? When I was first divorced, I got a part-time job as a bookkeeper and controller of this movie production company. My boss was a mail catalog addict and would spend his days browsing through catalogs and buying things he didn't need that his wife would secretly return.

"Please call Henri Bendel in New York to see if my suit is ready," he asked me one day.

I called 411 and got the number for Henri Bendel, dialed it, and asked the woman who answered the phone, "May I speak with Henri Bendel, please?

She slammed down the phone on me. How was I supposed to know that Henri Bendel was a store on Fifth Avenue? I just thought it was some guy named Henri. It was like calling Macy's and asking, "May I speak to Macy please?" I still laugh at my own stupidity. Always laugh at yourself before others get a chance to laugh at you. It will help keep you young and happy.

Silly Childhood Fun. One of my fondest memories is when my parents took us to Miami Beach every year to some old rickety hotel on Collins Street that had watermelon eating contests and a "funniest costume" contest for the kids. I was very fair skinned, so I was always sunburnt and looked like a lobster. (I won the funniest costume contest, and I wasn't even wearing a costume.)

My parents took us to New York every year. We always stayed in this tiny apartment with our old grandparents who were from Europe. It was across the street from Bronx Park and my first memory of their apartment was looking outside the window and watching the bums pee in the park.

My grandparents didn't talk to me, probably

because they didn't speak English, but I do remember my grandfather's false teeth soaking in a glass in the only bathroom. (I was afraid to go in the bathroom because I was frightened that they would bite me.) The subway ran under the bedroom every five minutes while I *tried* to sleep. I spent the nights in a bed that was jumping around the room like a Mexican jumping bean, hanging on for dear life to the headboard, trying to stay in the bed until the next train passed under my bed. It happened all night long. I think this may be the reason I still sleep half-hanging over the side of the bed.

I remember my Aunty Dora and her funny-looking synthetic wig. My mother used to make me put on my pink satin ballet tutu and dance for Aunty Dora and my grandparents. I wasn't that cute, and it was clear I wasn't going to become a prima ballerina. Aunty Dora lived with my grandparents until they died. In those days they called her an old maid, but nowadays a woman who never got married is called too picky, but I suspect there're are other reasons. Aunty Dora was tiny and always getting mugged in the Bronx, so she packed up her wigs and moved to California to be with my mother after my grandparents died. Of course, the first week she got there, she got mugged.

The Stupid Things We Believed. I love to laugh at how naïve I was when I was little. My mother would tell me that "They roll the sidewalks in at night." I was only five years old, so I refused to go out at night. I spent my days trying to figure out where they put the wheels on the sidewalks. I hadn't been to California yet and still thought a mango was a Latin dance and the tooth fairy was Liberace. (Well, my parents called him a fairy.) She also told me that if I didn't eat all my vegetables the Boogey Man would get me. It would have been easier if my mother had realized she was supposed to cook the frozen vegetables. I was afraid of the Boogey Man, and I still am. These are kind of good nostalgic memories of growing up. Let's keep these memories in our Good Memory Box. We don't need to lock it because it's great to be able to open it up anytime we need to feel good and laugh at ourselves. *Laughing stirs up our endorphins and makes our worries go away.*

CHAPTER EIGHTEEN
Dating for The Young at Heart

YOU'RE NEVER TOO old to have fun and enjoy life. You may think you are, but you're wrong. It can happen to anyone, including you, if you have a positive and *realistic* attitude about finding a mate and putting yourself out there in the world. It's never too late to fall in love. I have a client whose mother just turned one hundred and has a boyfriend at her assisted living home. There are many places to find a new mate once you decide to stay young and be happy.

Dating Sites and Apps. First you try Tinder for a while, but then you find out it's for having a marital affair and you don't have anyone to cheat on and you get carpal tunnel syndrome from Tinder anyway. Then you try Fling but find out Flinging is a crazy new sport in China that involves flinging yourself over obstacles. Your hips and knees won't take it. You think about joining eHarmony, but you can't sing. Then you get hip and join OkCupid, but your eyesight is going, your hands shake, and you accidentally sign up for OkStupid. *That doesn't work out so well. Don't give up!*

Blind Dates. Whether you're single, newly divorced or widowed—or whatever, friends and relatives like to fix you up. Blind dates are an excellent way to find a new mate, but you'll have to kiss a few frogs to find a prince, or princess. People have their own personalities and interests, and you need to find someone that matches yours.

I have a theory about who will connect with who. It is a way of matching people that will click together. It has to do with specific attributes and flaws that make all people different. It is a rating system of one to ten. The closer you are to the other person's number, the better the possibility that you will both connect. Here are a few of the attributes you need to consider before getting into or continuing a relationship with another person.

Physical attraction is the most important. If you feel like a magnet is pulling you to kiss and touch this person, it may just be the real thing. If you can't even bring yourself to kiss the other person, it's a no-go.

Sense of humor is the second most important. If you don't have the same sense of humor, it just won't work. If something makes you start laughing hysterically and the other person looks at you as if you're crazy, move on.

Lifestyle is the third most important component of

a relationship. If one person loves hiking and dreams of climbing Mount Everest and the other likes fancy hotels and restaurants, and dreams of going to on a luxury trip to Monaco, it probably won't work.

Political views are the fourth in importance. If one person is a radical right-wing liberal and the other person is a radical left-wing conservative, it won't work either. You'll both spend your lives screaming at each other.

Children are important too. If one person hates children, especially yours, it's a big issue. If one person wants to have children and the other one doesn't, it's a major issue. If you both don't have the same goals, it's a deal-breaker.

Money can make or break a relationship. If you don't agree how much money you need or how to spend it, you'll both be on a slippery slope.

Here are just a few of the many *flaws* in people that should send you back to watching re-runs of Gilligan's Island all weekend.

Liars and Cheaters. After my divorce, a friend fixed me up with The Stallion, a special effects guy in the movie industry and a recent widower. He was a fabulous dancer and would take me to wrap parties like the one for the movie "Bullet" where we would dance while the whole cast of Bullet gathered around clapping and screaming "Go Mo Go!" I felt like a wet mop being dragged around the dance floor.

One night The Stallion slept over. He had been a pyrotechnics expert in the service which turned out to be a lifesaver. I had forgotten to turn off the light over the fish tank and woke up at 5:30 am to a strong smell of smoke. I ran into the kitchen where flames were shooting up everywhere. The Stallion was nonchalantly wetting towels and placing them over the flames calmly while I screamed hysterically. Once the flames had subsided and I couldn't breathe through the smoke, I saw all of my beautiful freshwater fish floating upside down on the top of my huge, gorgeous aquarium. I wasn't sure if they were all dead or just doing the backstroke. For that moment, he was a hero. But wait…

I had joined his poker group, which had been his poker group with his deceased wife. Well, she wasn't deceased when she played poker with them, *at least I don't think so.* I was picking him up to go to the poker group together and, unexpectedly, he was waiting outside his house for me. I had some red flags and a hunch about some girl who was always leaving phone messages on this answering machine, so I called his number the next day, and a woman's voice answered, "Hello.". That was that. *Once a cheater, always a cheater.*

Zero Attraction. The next blind date came to the door to pick me up wearing an Elvis hairdo and a burgundy red and chartreuse striped velvet sports jacket with dust on it. (I confess, I'm very shallow deep down.) I had to go to a movie with him. I think it was the "Texas Chainsaw Massacre." As we crossed the street to the movie theater, he tried to take my hand, but I was scared somebody I knew would see me, so I pretended I wasn't with him. Thank God the movie theatre was dark. If you're embarrassed—and shallow—to be seen with someone, they're not for you.

No Sense of Humor. Another blind date was a very nice guy and owned a ticket agency for all the concerts and shows in Los Angeles. On our first date, he took me to see a Bette Midler concert and the usher showed us to our seats, front row center. We sat down and I whispered jokingly, "Couldn't we get any better seats?" He looked at me as if he wanted to stab me. Apparently, he didn't get my sense of humor. And that was the end of that. *The same sense of humor is a must!*

Alcoholics. I had a few dates with alcoholics and drug addicts. One guy had too many drinks on our date and thought he was driving in a bumper car. He hit too many curbs for a second date. The other was the host of a huge event for the entertainment industry and the room was full of old celebrities. I was left to sit at the table with two old movie stars, both of whom had nothing to say to me, while he stumbled up on the stage with a bright red face and slurred his way through the awards he was giving out. What awards, I don't remember, probably for the best facelifts. There were others addicts. *My advice: Stay Away.* There are many other places to meet new friends and possible mates.

Wine Tastings can be a good place to meet someone to date or even a new mate. It's like a smorgasbord of every gender designation. They are great places to meet people of all ages even if you don't know the difference between beer and champagne other than the price. Warning: This can also be a place to meet an alcoholic or a phony too. Be careful.

Art Fairs are wonderful outdoor events and are a great way to talk to new people. There are lots of handmade treasures to enjoy and maybe even buy. There are also a lot of single people wandering around on the grass. Maybe you'll stumble into someone interesting.

Book Signings at your local bookstore or library are where authors come in to promote their new books and read passages. You can chat with the author after and have them sign their book for you. They are great places to meet other people of all sexes and ages that you can converse with about the book. Just don't talk about politics. It's the great divider.

Garden Tours are a wonderful way to enjoy all the colors in nature and the smell of roses. (I'm not sure what the opposite sex is any more. A garden tour is a wonderful way for all of us nature-starved people to spend a day. It will make us feel happy. Actually, so will the wine tasting, too.

Architectural Tours are another great way to meet a potentially significant other. (If a "significant other" only refers to a mate of a different sex does that make your mate of the same sex an "insignificant other"?) There are a lot of beautiful and interesting homes and buildings in most cities to see, and you never know whom you will meet. It could be a wonderful person or an ax murderer. (Ax murderers like interesting architecture too, or they're scouting out places to bury their bodies.) These tours involve a lot of walking, so even if you don't meet someone, you'll get some good exercise.

Cooking Classes are a wonderful way to meet someone who likes to cook. A great place for us women to find a man who will cook for us. Cooking is *so over* for us aging females, but we love to eat. You can tell by our stomachs and rear-ends. Men who know how to cook don't even need a penis. Just a good set of pots and pans and cooking utensils will work. (Maybe there's a way to have sex with cooking utensils. *Probably*.)

Health Clubs have lots of interesting co-ed exercise classes to take. There are yoga classes for seniors: Downward Facing Dog (if your doctor said it was okay to bend your head below your heart), Frog Pose (if you haven't had knee replacements and are about to croak), and Cobra (if your arms are strong enough to lift your body. Health clubs also have salsa dancing, although I think it's kind of messy to dance in salsa, and kickboxing, for angry people who have pent up anger.

Joining a health club is a great way to meet other single people of all ages. There is nothing sexier than an older woman lifting weights with her batwing arms swinging or looking up older men's gym shorts while they're doing sit-ups.

Most health clubs have water exercises for older people. You men will love watching the ladies floating with their swan inner tubes and bicycling their legs in the water and you women will love watching the men swim across the pool with their swim fins and goggles before the lifeguard has to save them.

Pickle Ball has become a great way to meet people and get some exercise. The only thing is that I can't figure out how you can swat pickles back and forth with a paddle without them getting squashed. And what kind of pickles do they use, sweet or dill? What if someone gets hungry and eats them all? How do you play? What if pickleball gets so popular it uses up all the world's pickle supply and there's a pickle shortage? Can you swat a gherkin? Gherkin-ball?

Tennis is fun if you can find a doubles game of tennis to join. There's nothing more wonderful than being a woman that has to wear one of those cute little tennis skirts with matching ruffled panties and bending down for all the men to see your cellulite and part of your tush hanging out. Men, please don't think your wobbly legs and knobby knees look too wonderful in those ugly white shorts either.

Golf is a lot better. At least you get to wear longer pants. It's a great way to meet new people and socialize if you don't mind hitting a tiny ball into a little cup all day in the hot sun. Older people get sunstroke easier, so wear your hat and sunscreen so the bald spots on your head won't get sunburned or your hair coloring won't fade. Wearing gloves is a good idea since your hands are the first place on your body to show aging, other than your genitals. (I think that's true, but I'm not sure.) Never give up. Get out there and try all the time. It only takes meeting one right person to change your entire life! You will find that person if you choose to stay young and happy.

CHAPTER NINETEEN
How to Find Love at Any Age

SENIOR LOVE IS better than young love. Young love is fleeting. Old love is forever. I'm willing to put up with much more because I know no one else will put up with me. We still hold hands when we walk together. That's because we are trying to keep each other from falling. It's so sweet. He wakes up in the morning and looks over at the bed and says, "I love you so much!" The problem is I don't know whether he's talking to me or our dog, Lulu.

Lou and I have a lot in common, like sense of humor, constipation, insomnia, and gas. I love how he saves money by refusing to buy new sweatpants, ever. He doesn't wear underwear at home to save laundry detergent and usually walks around holding his pants up with one hand since the elastic is not elastic anymore and the drawstrings are broken. Sometimes, when he needs both hands to bring me an English muffin in the morning, but by the time he gets to me, his pants have fallen down to the floor. It's so cute! And I always know which room he's in because there is a trail of spilled coffee leading to it. It's a good thing he's not running from the FBI.

Finding love or finding love again when you're older is hard, I admit, but growing old alone is harder. When you find a mate that has the same sense of humor as you, you laugh together, and your life becomes more joyful. When you can talk with your mate about your deepest thoughts and share intimate moments, you have a treasure. As you age together and go through life's ups and downs, you will find yourselves taking care of each other. You both find your true happiness together (or hate each other's guts.) Love at any age is about feeling one hundred percent comfortable with each other.

When you were young and a guy you really like hadn't called you back for a second date it was living hell waiting for him to call and it usually meant he didn't like you. When you're older, if a man doesn't call you for a second date, it's because he lost your phone number and can't remember where you live, much less your name, or got lost going home, or had a heart attack and died. Check the obituaries before you feel rejected. If you're a guy, you probably remember a time when you finally got up the courage to call a girl for a date and she laughed and hung up the phone on you. As a single older man, now you call a woman and ask her out and she says, "What time should I pick you up?" because you don't drive anymore.

Your first date is going to the Senior Citizens Center to play canasta and drink grape punch. It's so much more exciting than going to a trendy restaurant and a Broadway Play.

Growing older should mean growing wiser. To finally know who should be in our lives and who shouldn't. Who makes us feel good about ourselves and who makes us feel bad about ourselves. The secret to aging happily is to surround yourself with only quality people who are on your team. Our family therapist kept on drumming into me about Fart King, "He's not on your team!" He's not on your team! HE'S NOT ON YOUR TEAM!!!!" she would scream at me. It was hard for me to understand when I was younger that someone who loved me so much once could have so much hate and vengeance for me now that he would want to kill me. It was one of the lessons in life I would have to learn to accept. Never underestimate the power of rejection.

I was lucky to have found love again. Lou was sitting across from me at Deli one memorable day. I saw that he ordered his eggs straight up, so that was a good omen. He was well-built nice-looking man with black hair and hazel eyes, eleven years older than me.

Our first date was at the top of the Holliday Inn on the 405 Freeway. (It actually wasn't *on* the 405 Freeway, or we would have gotten run over.) I didn't like his comb-over and glasses, but I was an interior designer then and knew he would make a good fixer-upper.

We dated for a while and then he decided we should introduce our daughters to each other. This was going to be a real experience since both of our kids were "difficult", which is to put it mildly. He takes us all to a Chinese restaurant and we order a bunch of items off the menu to share family style. His eighteen-year-old daughter is babbling on about her crush on some actor while my twelve-year-old daughter is sitting there with this Frau Farbissina look on her face, refusing to eat. The waiter comes over and asks her, "Don't you like your food?"

"No," she answered. "It tastes like shit." It was one of her more well-behaved moments.

"Oh, I'm sorry, "We'll make sure you get something you like more next time" the waiter apologizes.

"There won't be a next time!" she shouts back at him.

Life hasn't always been easy for a lot of us. We both knew life was going to be challenging for us after that dinner at the Chinese restaurant. My fortune cookie had no fortune in it.

Lou moved in with me. The big problem, other than our two daughters, was the fleas. Lou was allergic to fleas, but they loved him. It wasn't a two-way relationship. The fleas multiplied faster than herpes at an orgy and I couldn't get rid of the little suckers. They were dancing all over Lou's legs.

"It's either Arthur or me!" he screamed at me.

"Just let me think about it a few days," I teased.

Arthur, our Bichon Frieze, weighed eight pounds

and had the penis the size of a hundred-pound Rottweiler. I could have kept Arthur and made a fortune with doggy pornos. Dogs like pornos, right?

Our wedding was simple and not too big, about seventy-five people at Le Hermitage restaurant. We met with our Spiritual Leader, who was going to perform our wedding ceremony the following week. We told him that both of our daughters were making a scene about whether they were coming to the wedding or not. I'm sure both of their motives were to drive us crazy and piss us off. As I told you earlier in the book, our Spiritual Leader told us, "No one, not even your children, has the right to make your life unhappy." I have lived by this wisdom ever since and it will serve all of us well if we want to stay young and happy forever.

One friend came to our wedding wearing his green swim fins. My mother showed up wearing a dress she had made in sewing class. The sleeves were sewn on backwards, but I didn't have the heart to tell her. She must have been very hungry before dinner was served because she wet her finger and swiped off some icing off the bottom of the wedding cake, then sucked it off her finger. What I didn't know yet was that she had Alzheimer's. My then thirteen-year-old daughter and her friend came with black eyeshadow ringed eyes and green spiked hair. It's not my fault, I promise; she was living with Fart King. Blame him. The waiters thought they were older than twenty-one, so they kept on serving them wine. I had two thirteen-year-old drunks at my wedding. I wasn't going to let that bother me. It was my day. Or was it?

Another good friend, Harvey, who had been the lead prosecutor in the Bob's Big Boy case, a famous bloodbath shotgun shooting at a Bob's Big Boy in West Los Angeles in which four people were killed and five others wounded. He had prosecuted the main shooter, who was convicted of four first-degree murders and sentenced to death. He escaped prison right before our wedding and was out to kill our friend. Harvey came to our wedding armed with a Glock and two armed security guards (I don't think there are any one-armed security guards) that were standing outside our wedding all night. This must have been an *omen*.

Lou and I had just moved into our dream condo by the ocean. A psychic had told me a few years after I was divorced from Fart King that I would meet a tall dark handsome man, marry him, and live in a townhouse by the ocean. Not that I believe in psychics, but she was actually right, and psychics are cheaper than psychiatrists, who are usually in psychotherapy themselves, not that psychics could need therapists too.

A few days later I was sitting in my office on the bottom floor office of our three-story condo with the shutters open, admiring the view, when I saw Fart King walk by the window. I thought it might be a mirage, but it felt more like a nightmare. He lived thirty miles away and like poop clinging to the bottom of my shoe, here he was. Turns out his psychiatrist

(God knows he needed one) lived in the condo next door. One flimsy wall separated his therapy session from me when I was in my office. He came in his chauffeur driven limousine (he got very wealthy after I signed the Divorce Settlement that screwed me out of millions of dollars) two or three times a week to see his psychiatrist. Don't think I didn't use the glass against the wall to try to listen. It didn't work. Maybe I should have used a real glass instead of a paper cup.

A few months later, while we were watching Sixty Minutes on TV, Lou and I saw a segment on Lois Lee and Children of the Night, which was an organization that got runaways off the streets of Hollywood and helped them get away from their pimps. We decided it would be a good thing for us to do for society, so we called Children of the Night and asked if we could volunteer. They did a background check on us, and we started training a few weeks later.

After we were trained, we worked the crisis lines and took phone calls 24/7 from kids in trouble. After a few weeks, we got a call from a girl that screamed into the phone, "I'm being held hostage by a pimp, please help me!" It turned out to be the daughter of a friend. Because we knew Lois Lee, we were able to get their daughter rescued, put her in a live-in program, and get her to turn her life around. She is thriving now. Our Guiding Spirit had guided us to volunteer for Children of the Night for this mission. *Again, there are no coincidences.*

The following year we went on a ski trip to

Squaw Valley and jumped into a six-seater gondola. Once the door was shut and the gondola was quickly on the way up a snow-covered mountain, I looked across from me and there was a little boy with a very snotty nose. He was sneezing and coughing, and the droplets were filling up the gondola and landing on my face. I had no scarf to protect my face.

Once home, I started getting sicker and sicker. It kept on getting worse and worse and I went from doctor to doctor for six months. One day I was in the shower and got dizzy and nauseas and went into uncontrollable seizures and shaking. I fell on the tile shower floor and crawled out. Luckily an interior design client of mine called. I crawled to the phone and asked her for help.

She called her husband, a urologist who bragged that he had replaced John Wayne Bobbitt's penis after his wife cut it off. Dr. Schlong got me into a hospital, where a neurologist took all kinds of tests including a spinal tap. I spent over a week there with tests until the results came in from the spinal tap. It was viral spinal meningitis. The neurologist was able to give me two courses of the right anti-viral and the convulsions and headaches slowly disappeared. What did I learn from this? Anything can happen to anyone at any time. There are no guarantees that nothing will ever happen to you. *Every day is a blessing. Live it to the fullest if you want to stay young and be happy.*

CHAPTER TWENTY
Vacations for Older People

TRAVELING NOWADAYS IS a challenge for most of us. You know I don't like being negative (*well ...er, maybe a little*) so I'm going to find the humor in traveling post pandemic. If you can't find the humor in it, just stay home, and watch re-runs of Seinfeld. Just keep on seeing the humor in life no matter where you are.

First you have to decide what kind of trip you want to go on. Then you have to find a place you want to see. Then you have to check if the weather will be good. Then you have to read about all the things you can do at this place. Then you have to figure out the dates. Then you have to find a nice hotel, motel. or Airbnb you like and can afford. Once you book a room you have to find a flight. There are just about no direct flights now, so you have to figure out how to catch the next flight without them taking off without you.

Okay, you got through this, now all you have to figure out is what you're going to wear since global warming has made guessing the temperature of any place almost impossible. You pack a little of everything; raincoat, galoshes, bathing suit, ski jacket, lightweight tops, sweaters, sneakers, dresses, jeans, boots, sandals, dress shoes, enough shampoo, conditioner, and body lotion and shampoo to take on a plane, which amounts to nine 3.4-ounce plastic bottles stuffed in one sandwich bag, which allows you to wash your hair and have a shower one time in two weeks. Being dirty can be fun. You can't even take some sandwiches on a plane. *Headline: Salami Sandwich Explodes and Brings Down Plane!*

You and your significant other of choice (in case you have several significant others) drive to the airport three hours ahead of time just to be safe, get stuck in freeway traffic for two hours, get to the airport parking lot, which has now switched to GetScrewed parking meters, which is great, because you paid online in advance, and you're assured a parking space. *Wrong.* Once you arrive, there are absolutely no parking spaces available. You try to get a refund from the parking attendant, but he doesn't speak English, or online at getscrewed.com, but their website is down. So, you try to find a valet to take your car after paying $500 to getscrewed.com in advance to park for two weeks in the airport lot.

Next, you go to the check-in machine to retrieve the tickets you bought online, but your paper tickets get stuck in the machine and there's no one to help you. Finally, you check in with mutilated tickets only to find out there's an hour wait in line to check in your baggage.

Finally, you get it all taken care of and go to the gate, only to find another hour wait at the security check line. You go through the X-ray scanner and the alarm goes off because of your penile or breast implants, so you have to go through a full body scan to see if you've got any drugs stuffed in your penis or boobs.

You eventually get to the gate and either your flight has left without you, it's been delayed twelve hours and you still have to wait, or it's been canceled, and you have to sleep on the airport floor all night and maybe even the next night until they get you another flight. You finally get on another flight, but the pilot looks stoned or drunk. What the hell, you think, we'll take a gamble. You wait another few hours in the plane on the tarmac and the pilot finally announces, "I'm sorry folks, but we're going to have a little bit of turbulence most of the way. We're heading into a few hurricanes. The plane ahead of us is going to go ahead first and we'll see if they make it." Bolts of lightning are hitting your plane as it sits on the tarmac. You're wondering if the people on the plane ahead of you are dead or alive.

The guy sitting next to you gets drunk and starts having a fight with the flight attendant and all hell breaks out. The passengers have to subdue the man sitting next to you and bandage him up in his seat with electrical tape. (Why do they carry electrical tape on a plane? Do they use it to tape on the wing if it starts to blow off.) So now you're sitting next to an out-of-control drunk man taped to his seat and the pilot announces, "Fasten your seat belts, we're in for a real ride." You've never prayed in your life, but all you can do now is down a few drinks and pray to any God that will listen to you. I don't know if that includes *God*zilla.

You're finally landing, the plane is touching down, and you sigh with relief until the pilot pulls the plane right back up again. You ask the flight attendant why the pilot pulled up, and she tells you "Oh, there was no one in the control tower. They're all on strike."

The pilot makes two or three more attempts to land the plane in the hurricane and finally makes it in. You're on your way to fun in the sun. It's pouring out and you're soaking wet. You get to your hotel and the front desk clerk tells you that they had to give your reservations away and there are no other rooms – in all of Florida. The hotels are all overbooked because of the Condom Convention in town.

When things were good, Lou and I took lots of trips. Lou's partner's wife was the self-proclaimed travel agent, but we always had her plan our trips anyway. This time we were going to Boston, Newport Rhode Island, Nantucket, and Martha's Vineyard. We wanted to see the beauty of the leaves falling off the trees, much nicer than watching our beautiful locks of hair falling out as we age. Sue had gotten us reservations in what she called "a darling little bed and breakfast in Nantucket." She didn't mention a bathroom, but we just assumed it had one. This is how I learned not to "assume" anything as I've aged. The little house was very cute so when we went inside to check in, I was still very seasick from the ferry we had taken over from Martha's Vineyard, so I just wanted a room to puke in. We didn't ask questions. *Big mistake.*

The owner of the bed and breakfast told us, "Since you're so late, we only have one room left, she said, as she showed us to our room. "It doesn't exactly have a bathroom *in* the room, but your private bathroom is just across the hallway from your room. Your room does have your own shower though." In order to use our bathroom, we had to put on our bathrobes and slippers and sneak across the hallway to avoid every other guest from seeing us. The good news, or sort of good news, was that our shower was actually in our room. They had taken a small closet, piped in some water, and hung up a shower curtain. Good thing we're thin. "I'm going to the closet for a shower honey" we would tell each other, laughing. What I learned from this was *always ask for details.*

Another time we went to Florida to see some friends and took a side trip to Savannah Georgia, which is known as the Fountain of Youth, but was more like the Fountain of Sweat it was so hot. It's also known for its haunted houses and ghosts, but I had never believed in ghosts, so it wasn't a problem. Sue had gotten us reservations for this cute bed and breakfast, and we got to our room. Lou went to bathroom to brush his teeth and walked out to ask me something. He had a glass in his hand and all of a sudden, the glass completely cracked into hundreds of pieces in his hand and fell to the floor. We were stupefied. Maybe I was starting to believe in ghosts now. It was confirmed when we moved into the Encino house years later.

Our Airedale, Charley, had developed kidney disease and started getting terribly sick, she wouldn't eat, she was too weak to walk and was in pain, so we had to put her down humanely. It was a horrible experience, and we were crestfallen.

Not long after she passed, I began seeing her in the house. She was a shadowy figure that I could walk through and yet I could swear she was there. There were a few other shadowy see-through dogs in our house that might possibly been the ghosts of dogs that had died in that house over the years. Then there was always a fisherman complete with a rubber raincoat and hood that fishermen wear. He was tall and thin and would always be by my bed looking out the window. I don't believe in ghosts I don't think, but I swear I saw these ghosts in our house in Encino. *Was I going crazy?* Once we moved to Las Vegas, the ghosts were completely gone. What I learned is that anything is possible, even ghosts, haunted houses, and UFO's.

Our next trip was to Puerto Vallarta where we sat around cozying up to each other in the pool when we weren't shopping for cheap silver jewelry. We would watch the Mexican workers wash windows and walls in the rain. At the hotel restaurant, we asked the waiter if he could get us some grass. He asked us if we'd like Kentucky Blue or AstroTurf. Neither of us liked Marijuana, but we heard that it was the thing to do in Mexico. *The person who told us that must have wanted us dead.*

We found some pot and went back to our room, got stoned, and then decided to take a walk on the beach in the dark. We were terrified and we thought we heard someone following us on the beach so we started running as fast as we could back to our room.

The next day we were bored, so we rented a Jeep and took a side trip to Ixtapa, ignoring the warnings of a Huracán, mostly because we didn't understand what it was. Ixtapa was great. We had lunch at this little café built up on a mountain that had the best pizza we ever ate and watched about one hundred cows being herded down the winding street by a man on a horse with a cow bell. Sometimes life really does give you cow dung!

We started back to our hotel in Puerto Vallarta, and it started clouding up, the wind was picking up, and it started to pour. We were in an open Jeep, so we took refuge outside a closed restaurant on the patio as the winds because violent and the rain became torrential and the beach chairs and umbrellas started flying in the air, barely missing us.

We decided to try to make it back to our hotel, which was still another sixty miles away. The rain was pouring into the open Jeep, we were soaking wet, but like true adventurers, we braved the hurricane and somehow made it back to our hotel soaking wet and laughing. The next morning, we decided to go to Acapulco. We found a little storefront in the village that had a sign on it that said, "Travel Agent," so we went in. *Sounds good, right? Think again.* The walls were plastered with travel posters, and we saw this sinister-looking man with yellow teeth sitting behind a big desk smiling at us. "Hola" he called out to us.

"We want to go to Acapulco tomorrow. Can you arrange a flight and a hotel for us?" Lou asked.

"I can drive you there and it would be mucho cheaper" he replied.

"Oh great! That would be an adventure," I said to Lou enthusiastically.

"What do we have to lose?" asked Lou hesitantly. *Maybe our lives?*

"Can you make reservations for us at The Princess Hotel too?' Lou asked the greasy little man.

"Of course!" exclaimed the travel agent. "For you, anything!"

This should have been a red flag.

The next morning it's about 100 degrees and the humidity is 99% and Eduardo, the Travel Agent from Hell, picks us up in his old rickety car. We put all our luggage in the dirty trunk that smelled like a dead body and climbed into the car. It smelled like burritos and nachos. *Maybe the dead body had eaten burritos and nachos before our driver killed him and stuffed him in the trunk.*

"It's hot as the basement of hell in here señor, can we please turn on the air conditioning?" I asked as my makeup was melting down my face like Rudy Giuliani at a press conference.

"Of course!" he said as he rolled down all the windows and smiled. "*Si,* air conditioning."

As we drove through all these little towns of unpaved streets with flat-headed women carrying fifty-pound clay jugs on their heads and vendors with carts of mystery meat, hours passed, and I had to pee. There wasn't a bathroom in sight. No Starbucks, no McDonalds. We had gone about one-third of the way to Acapulco and now we see a roadblock. *Uh Oh.* It's lined with black *Policía Federali* wearing black moustaches and long barreled guns slung over their shoulders.

Eduardo stops the car and turns his head to the backseat. "No worry, I take care of this *leetle* situation," he assures us as the *Policía Federali* yanked him out of the car and forced him to open up his trunk.

"The grass" I whisper to Lou. "It's in the trunk." His face turned white, and then dropped to the floor like a bag of wet cement. I visualized spending the rest of my life in some concrete filthy prison cell eating rat tacos and getting raped by toothless dirty men.

Then they pulled us out of the car and made us stand by the trunk as two or three *Policía Federali* rummaged through our suitcases with the barrels of their guns. We watched as they all looked at my big box of tampons. I was about to faint. *We were going*

*to spend the rest of our lives in a Mexican prison, I
knew it!*

"Okay, good to go," said one of the *Policía
Federali* as he slammed the trunk shut.

I thanked God I hadn't gone through menopause
yet and we got back into the rear seat. I sigh relief
and whisper to Lou, "The grass was in the bottom of
the tampon box."

We drive through more small towns with cobble
stone streets and the Travel Agent from Hell turns
to the back and asks us, "You like lobster? I have
a cousin who owns a lobster restaurant right on the
beach."

"Sounds good if they have a bathroom," I say as
I cross my legs tighter.

"Yes, señorita!"

The Travel Agent from Hell turns right onto an
old dirt and rock road and keeps on driving for a few
more miles until he makes another right onto this
very narrow road filled with dense jungle on either
side. He keeps on driving longer and longer on this
dirty, rocky road, getting us deeper and deeper into
this eerie thick jungle.

"I think he's going to kill us," I whisper to Lou.

"Maybe," he whispers back.

*At least "maybe" was more consoling than "I'm
positive."*

We go further on further down the narrow dirt
road until it turns into sand, and then a big shanty
kind of house appears and lots of men that look like
Mexican Mafia start running towards the car calling

out "Hola, Hola, Hola!" The travel agent either has a very big family of relatives or these are the Mexican Mafia running out to rob us, cut us up in little pieces, and throw us in the ocean, or maybe they we just calling me a whore.

"Have we got lobster for we!" they were yelling. I thought maybe "lobster" was a code word for machete. I remembered that lobsters never age, they live long because they are organisms that are able to grow without aging. That is why lobsters can live longer than many other animals, except turtles, who can live to be over 200 years old. So maybe this was a good omen. Maybe lobsters hold the secret to longevity? *I don't know.* But how do they know this? Most lobsters spend their lives in fish tanks waiting to get boiled alive and eaten. This is animal cruelty. Lobsters have feelings too. We need to stop this.

I get out of the car and the herniated disks in my neck are making a crunching noise like a coffee grinding machine. A fat woman with bag wings flapping under her upper arms comes running out waving two live lobsters in her hands. "Hola! Hola! Hola!" I thought maybe she was calling me a whore too. Maybe we were the dinner, who knows? As it turns out, it was a wonderful lobster dinner, I got to pee, and we had a wonderful time and couldn't wait to get the hell out of there before dark. Maybe they were fattening us up for the slaughter. We say "Gracias, gracias" and "Adios, adios," to our hosts of sorts and climb back into the car, make the long trip through the dirt road through the jungle while my herniated disks clashed together like castanets and we're on our way to Acapulco. *Yay! At least, I think*.

The Travel Agent from Hell drives up to the lobby door of The Princess Hotel and pulls our suitcases out of the trunk, places them on the driveway and drives off as fast as he can. *This should have been a red flag too*. We pick up our suitcases and traipse into the lobby and over to the front desk.

"Reservations for Rima Rudner please," I tell the clerk at the front desk, who fumbles all over the desk and looks into this prehistoric computer over and over again and then fumbles through some more papers. No reservations for Rima Rudner, señorita," he tells us, not really giving a rat's ass that we're going to be homeless in Acapulco.

"Well, do you have any room for us?" I asked nicely.

"No, señorita, we're all booked up."

Lou pulls out a hundred-dollar bill and hands it to him.

"Let me see what I can find for you," he says.

"Make sure it has a bed," Lou says, handing him another hundred-dollar bill.

"Yes, Señor, two" he assures Lou. "Oh, someone just checked out I see," exclaims the clerk. "The room has a nice ocean view."

We get to the room exhausted and plop down on the two twin beds. We're too tired to worry about the fact the toilet doesn't flush and we're next to the elevator shaft and the garbage chute.

The next night I drag Lou to my favorite disco

in Acapulco, Babyos, even though he can't hear a beat and has three left feet. (Well, he hangs left.) Our cab pulls up to the front of the disco and there's a line waiting to get in four people wide and wrapped around the block. Lou gets pissed and refuses to wait in line so I said, "don't worry," taking a chance that they actually remembered me from the last time I was there with my girlfriend. I pulled Lou out of the cab, took him by the hand, and walked him under the red velvet rope that the two security guards held up for us as if we were Prince Charles and Diana and went right into the disco, where the maître d' escorted us to the prime table on the edge of the dance floor where all the A-list locals hung out. I was very proud of myself. My girlfriend and I must have made quite an impression. *I think I remember why.*

Lou and I drank Tequila poppers and Margueritas until we were pretty high and decided to call a cab and get back to the hotel, but before we could call a cab our new friend we had met at the disco, Rodney, as us "Where you guys stayin'?"

"We're at The Princess," Lou replies.

"We're stayin' there too," he says. We'll give y'all a ride back."

Rodney was wearing a black fedora hat and zoot suit with a fur collar. His girlfriend had huge breasts that looked like ripe honeydew melons and wore a red sequined mini dress with red stilettos to match a red feather boa. In a few minutes a valet pulls up in a white Cadillac convertible with chrome wheels spinning with lights, a fringed trimmed front window, all kinds of sparkly chains hanging from the rear-view mirror, and a huge gold eagle hood ornament pulls up. We hop in the back seat having a bad time sliding over on the fur covered seat covers, and we're on our warm balmy way back to The Princess Hotel with Rodney and Honeydew Boobs.

"So, what do you do for a living?" I asked Rodney, just to make conversation.

"I dibbles and I dabbles," he replied.

Lou elbowed so hard to shut up that I think he broke a rib.

CHAPTER TWENTY-ONE
Forty Ways Feel Happier and Younger

1. Accept that you can't make people love you if don't like or love yourself. Learn to like and love yourself by accepting the real you, flaws and all, and being kind to everyone, even your enemies.

2. Accept that you cannot make anyone love you, or even like you if they just don't. Let it go. Let them go. It's their loss.

3. Accept that you have limitations based on your own physical and mental abilities. Don't believe the myth that you can do anything you want to do in life. It's not true for most people. Just do what you love to do, as long as it doesn't hurt any living being. (Plants flowers don't count, they just look at me and die. I'm a foliage serial killer.)

4. Accept that everyone, including you, is always

aging from the day they are born. Know when you can no longer do the things you used to do. Listen to your body and learn to enjoy the things that your body will let you do (like get up three or four times a night to pee.)

5. Accept the things you don't have in your life. Enjoy the good things you do have. Material possessions will only make you happy until you get bored and tired of them and want even more. Remember, true friends, family, and personal achievements, no matter how big or small, will make you happy most of the time (except maybe at Thanksgiving.)

6. Accept that some people have left your life. Good friends may pass through your life, some move away, some move on, and some die, but *best friends* will stay with you for life, even if it's only good memories of them. Good memories will make you happy. Bad memories will make you unhappy. Let them go.

7. Accept change. Life is always evolving. As we get older, life moves faster, sometimes faster than we can keep up with, especially technology. Don't think you have to understand it all. You're not alone.

8. Accept that, unfortunately, good *and* evil live together on this planet. Hateful and corrupt people will probably roam the earth forever. Remember that the conflict between good and evil is our Creator's game of chess. Our Creator may have

intended to make our lives difficult-but-spell-binding, like a good movie.

9. Accept truth and reality. The truth is that our lives and our situations may not be ideal. The reality is that we all have our limitations. Relax and find joy and gratitude for the life you have. Count your blessings, not your misfortunes, and you will be at peace with yourself and the world. Peace will keep you young and happy.

10. Believe that everyone, including you, has their own special talents. Find out what your talents are and spend your time and energy perfecting them. Just do one thing to make the world a better place before you leave it.

11. Remember that timing is everything in life. Before you make a decision that could change your life, make sure your timing is right. It could mean the difference between losing and winning, even the difference between life and death. One split second could change your life. Stay safe and be wise, cautious, and vigilant.

12. Find new things to do that you *can do*. You don't have to be the best at anything. You can be a mediocre artist, but oil painting can make you happy. You like to play bridge but lose all the time, but you don't want to give up the social interaction. All you have to do is enjoy what you are doing, and you will stay young and happy.

13. Listen to your intuition, it is your Guiding Spirit fine-tuning your brain so that you can hear the little pings that alert you to stay away

from situations that won't end well, like buying a timeshare or investing in a cryptocurrency company that collapses. Stay informed.

14. Pay attention to red flags, your Guiding Spirit is waving them at you to keep you from getting swindled out of your money by some con man who offers you a big return on your money. Liars and cheaters are betting that you aren't hip to them. Learn to quickly spot the tricks liars and cheaters use.

15. Heed your omens, they are messages from your Life Concierge that will keep you from making bad decisions, like signing some papers you regret signing or ending up with someone abusive.

16. There are no coincidences, they are divine chance meetings arranged by your Guiding Spirit. Coincidences are what saved my life when I had cancer and led me to the only doctor on earth that could cure me. It is my Guiding Spirit that led me to create a new business that supported us for many years. Good things happen to people who recognize their coincidences as their Guiding Spirit and act on them right away. It just takes one quick stroke of good luck to completely change your life for the better. Learn to spot good luck quickly and grab it.

17. Socialize. Isolation breeds loneliness, illness, dementia, and death. The morgue isn't fun. Go mingle with good people if you want to feel alive and stay young and happy. Good people can be

found doing good things for the world. Let go of your fears and go join them.

18. Be grateful for whatever and whomever you have in your life. Treat them with the kindness and caring that you demand from others. No longer let toxic people ruin your happiness no matter how hard they try—and they will.

19. Change your thoughts of hate into thoughts of love and compassion. Every time you want to do or say something mean or hateful, process it through your brain and turn it into sympathy and empathy. Brainwash your own brain to think kinder thoughts.

20. Never hurt another person or animal. If you're about to say something to someone that may hurt them, stop, think, and shut up. As previous generations told us, "If you can't say anything nice, don't say anything."

21. Do something kind for someone every day. It's an exercise for your soul. Give a homeless person some money. Volunteer at a soup kitchen. Help an older person in a wheelchair get through a door or pay for the groceries of a veteran in line in front of you at the market. Kindness will always boomerang back to you tenfold.

22. Smile more. Shout less. You'll have more friends, and you'll do your larynx a favor. It will also keep you calmer and keep your blood pressure down, thus keeping you younger and happier.

23. If you want to achieve youth and happiness

forever, exercise your body and your mind every day. Use it or lose it.

24. Lies poison our souls. Don't tell lies and untrue stories. You'll always get caught and be thought of as a fool, even if you are one.

25. Truth sets our souls free. Genuineness gives us integrity, credibility, and respect. It also blesses us with the freedom of not having to try to remember the lies and stories we've already told.

26. Animals are here to teach us how to love. Humans are here to remind us that some people can be flawed. We are all flawed. No one is perfect. Toxic people can be more than flawed, they can be evil. If you choose to stay young and be happy, let go of the toxic people in your life if you can.

27. Love is very healing. A warm real hug, not a therapy hug, can heal emotional pain. When someone hugs you, it makes you feel warm and safe. When you hug someone, it makes you feel kind and caring. It's a win-win gift you can give to others, and it doesn't cost a penny.

28. Laughter is the fountain of youth. Never stop laughing or you will lose your youth and joy. Laugh *at* yourself, laugh *with* others, laugh at your flaws, laugh at your life, laugh at life itself.

29. Words are cheap. Actions are priceless. Let your actions, not your mouth, do the bragging. Don't give to charity to impress people. Give from your heart, it will make you happier.

30. If you can't laugh at yourself, what can you laugh

at? Laughing *with others is good* but laughing *at others is mean*. Never embarrass someone or try to make them feel bad about themselves. When you are mean, you are just degrading yourself in the hearts and minds of others.

31. Your soul is ageless. Your body, not so much. Take good care of it. You have one body. Treat it like it's a fine piece of furniture. If you want to stay *young*, eat healthily and exercise your mind and body. If you want to stay *happy*, be kind, help others, and laugh.

32. Never give up! Every time you think about killing yourself, remember that tomorrow may be your lucky day. What if you miss your lucky day? And if you're still worrying about what you're wearing when the paramedics find your body, you're really not ready to die yet.

33. Hate of others is really the hate of yourself. Learn to love yourself, flaws, and all, and you'll learn to love others and their flaws too. (Okay, I admit, there are some people that you'll probably never love, so just tolerate them.)

34. Pain is a reminder to take care of our precious bodies inside and out. It can be hard to stay young and happy if you are in pain, I know. Seek the right medical help and regimen to lessen your pain and keep focusing on your purpose in life. Purpose can get you through the pain. A meaningful goal may cure the pain.

35. Joy is the appreciation for the gift of life, the

beauty of Mother Nature, and giving to others while we try to achieve our purpose in life.

36. Purpose is the engine of our lives. Some of us are riding in the caboose and have to work harder, but no matter how old you are, please don't lose your purpose, it's the gasoline in the engine of hope.

37. Despair is the dark before dawn. It's also another reason not to consider killing yourself. What if you miss the one big opportunity in your life by killing yourself too soon? What if you devastate the people that love you? One chance meeting, one phone call, one email, one text message, can change your life situation for the better. In the meantime, just buy lottery tickets. It works to keep you hoping you'll win the next day. Never give up and you will never think of yourself as a failure.

38. Money is a necessity to live, it is also a way to help others. If you can't afford to give money, give with your time, energy, and spirit. Giving feeds our souls.

39. Depth is where we can find our true selves. It is where our happiness or sadness lies. It is where we feel young and vital or old and useless. Search your soul. You will find the strength you need to unlock your happiness and youthfulness. Your soul will guide you to find the joy and beauty of life and people.

40. Kindness is when we share our true selves. We unveil our sagging boobs and rear-ends,

our balding heads, our corns and bunions, our dental implants, our cellulite, our wrinkles, and the whole f--king mess we've become, and we still tell each other that we look beautiful and handsome. That's what growing old together means!

In Summary...

When we're older, we get to become the person that we have always wanted to be, but not if we allow ourselves to become the person we never wanted to be. We finally know what really makes us happy and feel at peace with ourselves. *Wisdom is the prize we get for living so long.*

Life is like a rollercoaster, it has its ups and downs, laughter and tears, thrills and fears. As we age, we learn a lot from each experience, but there is always more to learn. We discover the truths about life on Earth, the clash between good and evil, but most of all, we find the purpose of why each of us was blessed with life. If we didn't have a purpose, our Creator wouldn't have put us here. I feel *my* purpose is to help others be happier as they struggle with the difficulties of aging. Whether *your* purpose is a book, a painting, a song, or just to make one person happy, your soul will leave beautiful flowers on this planet in your memory. If you want to stay happy forever, always try to wake up with a purpose and a smile on your face no matter what is happening in your life or the world. Smile, laugh, think kind thoughts, and your heart and true happiness will follow. Never take your gift of life for granted.

Don't take every event so seriously. Good and bad things happen every day as sure as the Earth rotates 360 degrees about every twenty-four hours. Life is problem solving. You solve one problem and the next one pops up. Events always become good or bad memories with time as new things happen. Some even become funny memories we can laugh at forever. Bad memories give us wrinkles and frown lines, good memories give us dimples and twinkly eyes. Toss those bad memories in your Bad Memory Bag if you want to stay happy and young forever. Always treasure your Good Memory Box.

Our human bodies are only the vessels we use to navigate our lives for a very short time in light years. Some live inside better-looking vessels, some have different color skin and hair, are smarter than us, aren't as smart as us, have great talents, but most have *some* talent. Some speak a different language from us, or come from a different culture, a different religion, but inside every vessel, there is a heart, brain, and soul and all of the same organs that we have. Okay, the genitals vary a little with gender, but inside every vessel, there is a human being, male, female, LGBTQIA, black, white, or any color skin, that has real feelings that can get hurt by people who have no tolerance, compassion, or empathy. If you understand this, and that we can all blossom together, you are one step closer to becoming happy forever. *Live and let live.*

Hate is not inborn. It is taught to us by our non-tolerant family or friends. Hating is an ugly way for anyone to go through life. *Hate is a choice* just as *happiness is a choice*. To hate others is to hate ourselves and the world. Our world is very divided now. "United we stand, divided we fall." We can't seem to get along together and are becoming more and more divided. No one person or group is all right or all wrong. Political parties and cults have become "teams" that think they have to win or lose no matter who they hurt. If there were no "teams", just people working together to unite our country and the world to make it all a better place to live, it would create nonjudgmental, peaceful dialogue, tolerance, and understanding of others' pain and point of view. We could move forward for the good of all.

As the world and human beings have evolved slowly in the last fifty years, animals have evolved quickly. They have a lot to teach us about pure love and kindness and how it can help us stay young and happy forever. Animals also teach us a lot about *tolerance*. In the animal world, giraffes used to just hang out with giraffes, penguins with penguins, and dogs hated cats. We see now that all breeds of animals have become good friends with each other. Dogs and cats now cuddle and sleep together, female dogs nurse kittens that have lost their mother, horses and goats run and play together, even birds and reptiles are bonding with humans. The great thing about pets is that they don't get mad at you if you're late or forget their birthday. They always forgive you no matter what. The human race can learn a lot from animals, except for lifting their legs on new sofas and licking themselves clean. All it takes to make them happy is to bring them home a new toy or play ball with them. They show love when they are treated with love, kindness, and respect for their feelings. Animals can teach us the power of love, kindness, respect and how to give it to each other. Animals teach us how to be happy.

Of course, there are also predators in the animal world that are just out for their own survival and prey on weaker animals. Dogs started out as wolves, and cats started out as tigers, but some have been domesticated and bred to be kind and loving. Unfortunately, there are lots of predators in our human world too. They are self-serving and don't care who they hurt. Perhaps they are necessary to keep our Creator's ultimate game of life in action, but we need to figure out a way to breed humans with kinder souls. *Good must triumph over evil!*

Here are some quotes I love from the now-deceased comedy legend, Joan Rivers.

"Life is a movie, and you're the star. Give it a happy ending."

"Nothing is yours permanently, so you better enjoy it while it's happening."

"When you can laugh at yourself, no one can ever make a fool of you."

"I wish I had a twin, so I could know what I'd look like without plastic surgery."

"Listen. I wish I could tell you it gets better. But it doesn't get better. You get better."

"I enjoy life when things are happening. I don't care if it's good things or bad things. That means you're alive."

"The only good thing about age is that sooner or later, all of the SOBs who dumped you are going to die.

"Keep moving. It's hard for old age to hit a moving target."

... *Joan Rivers*

THE END

Biography

Rima Rudner
Published Author, Ghostwriter and Happiness Coach

HAPPINESS COACH, RIMA Rudner, is the published author of "Choose to Be Happy: A Guide to Total Happiness", Choose Inc. Publishing, 2008, which sold over 10,000 copies very quickly in the United States and foreign rights in many countries.

She is also the published author of "The Complete Guide to Decorating Your Home" authored as Rima Kamen (Betterway Publications, 1989, now P&W) as well as the co-author of "Who Moved My Birthday: The Baby Boomer's Essential Guide to Anti-Aging," with Dr. Brad Frank, MD, MPH, MBA, Dr. Sanjay Gupta, MD, and Richard Moon, RPh, FIACP.

Rima has written many screenplays, sitcoms, standup comedy routines, children's books, and magazine articles. Her ghostwriting includes other self-help books on health, diet and fitness, anti-aging, psychology, and relationships. You can view some of Rima's writing accomplishments at rimarudner.com. She writes in an easy-to-read, casual, and humorous style that most anyone can enjoy.

Rima has become a happiness coach for many prominent people. Having survived a highly dysfunc-tional family, an abusive first marriage, life-threat-ening ski accident, viral spinal meningitis, bladder cancer, financial disaster —and much more—she knows how to turn her life tragedies into learning experiences for us all. Throughout "Aging-itis", she explains how living through literally dozens of tragedies has made her stronger and happier and gives her the credentials to teach others how to be happy in spite of any and all adversities.

Rima was born in New York, lived in Chicago until she was thirteen, then moved to Los Angeles with her family when her father, a radiologist, was diagnosed with cancer. He died when she was twenty-one. She attended University High School, Santa Monica College, and then attended UCLA Design Program while raising her young daughter and working at Phyllis Morris Design, one of the popular design firms in Los Angeles. Her first job was working on the well-known author, Harold Robbins, house. She then opened her own design firm, Rima Kamen Interiors, and was a successful residential and commercial interior designer in Beverly Hills, Brentwood, Hollywood, Malibu, and Pacific Palisades. In 2008, when the stock market and real estate market crashed, her second husband lost his auto parts business, and she lost her design business, so Rima wrote her successful book, "Choose to Be Happy: A Guide to Total Happiness".

In order to survive the 2008 Recession, Rima started selling some of her things on eBay. Her wealthy friends who were in the same boat started giving her all their expensive designer bags, shoes, clothing, and accessories to sell online for them. Boxes of designer items would arrive daily. Then her buyers started asking her to sell their designer items for them.

Fast forward, Authentic Designer Stuff became one of the best design resale stores on the Internet and she had eight online stores in different countries. Unfortunately, after the 2016 election, her international sales started dwindling because the value of the dollar went up. By 2018, her sales had dwindled 75% and she and her husband moved to Las Vegas to lower their living costs.

By 2022, Rima started writing her newest book, "Aging-Itis: How to Find Happiness Despite It All". She now lives in Las Vegas with her second husband, Harvey, and her toy cockapoo, Lulu. *Lulu is a real dog, not a toy.*

Contact Rima:
rimarudner@gmail.com
www.rimarudner.com